Tax Law and Digitization

Tax Law and Digitization

How to Combine Legal Tech and Tax Tech

Edited by

Michael Lang
Robert Risse

Wolters Kluwer

Published by:
Kluwer Law International B.V.
PO Box 316
2400 AH Alphen aan den Rijn
The Netherlands
E-mail: lrs-sales@wolterskluwer.com
Website: www.wolterskluwer.com/en/solutions/kluwerlawinternational

Sold and distributed by:
Wolters Kluwer Legal & Regulatory U.S.
7201 McKinney Circle
Frederick, MD 21704
United States of America
E-mail: customer.service@wolterskluwer.com

ISBN 978-94-035-4313-0

e-Book: ISBN 978-94-035-4314-7
web-PDF: ISBN 978-94-035-4315-4

Editors

Univ.-Prof. Dr. DDr. h.c. Michael Lang is the head of the Institute for Austrian and International Tax Law at WU (Wirtschaftsuniversität Wien, the Vienna University of Economics and Business), and Academic Director of the LLM Program in International Tax Law and of the Doctorate Program in International Business Taxation (DIBT) at that university.

Prof. Dr. Robert Risse, lawyer and financial advisor, has been the head of the Tax and Trade department of Henkel AG & Co. KGaA since 2000 and is globally responsible for all topics and projects related to taxation and customs. From 1991 to 1998, Prof. Dr. Risse was responsible for corporate group management in the areas of national and international tax law in the tax department of Mannesmann AG, and from 1997 to 1999 was head of the Tax and Risk Management department of Deutsche Post AG. Prof. Dr. Risse is, among other things, on the board of the Rhein-Ruhr Discussion Group of the International Fiscal Association (IFA) (so-called IFA West), and is a member of the tax advisory examining board at the Ministry of Finance of North Rhine-Westphalia. Since August 2017, he has been Honorary Professor for Tax Compliance and Applied Tax Planning at the Institute of Accounting, Finance and Taxation at the University of Leipzig, Germany, chaired by Prof. Carmen Bachmann. Since December 2017, he has been the chairman of the board of directors for the WU Transfer Pricing Center at the Institute for Austrian and International Tax Law, WU (Vienna University of Economics and Business).

Contributors

Prof. Dr. Walter Brenner joined St. Gallen University in 2001 as a professor after having held the Chair of Information Systems at the University of Essen (Germany) for two years, and at Freiberg University of Mining and Technology (Germany) for seven years. Currently, Professor Brenner acts as Managing Director of the Institute of Information Management. From 2010 to 2012 he was Dean of the School of Management at the University of St. Gallen. His research focuses on Industrialisation of Information Management, Management of IT, Innovation and Technology Management. He authored and/or edited 30 books as well as more than 300 scientific publications. Professor Brenner received a graduate degree in business administration (lic. oec.) and a Doctorate (Dr. oec.) from the University of St. Gallen. Prior to joining academia Professor Brenner worked as Head of Application Development with Alusuisse-Lonza AG (Switzerland).

Matthias Gries, StB, graduated from the Otto-Friedrich University of Bamberg, Germany, with a doctorate in business taxation. He works as in-house tax advisor in the Tax Digitalization/VAT department at Siemens, and also as a lecturer at the University of Bamberg. Mr Gries previously worked as a tax advisor for Flick Gocke Schaumburg.

Benjamin Hils studied Economics at the University of Constance and has been working for the Handelsblatt Media Group in various areas since 2012. Among other things, he was Head of the Legal, Business and Tax Division of Handelsblatt Fachmedien. In this role, Benjamin Hils founded one of the leading tax technology conferences in Germany. He is the initiator of the Handelsblatt Media Group tax initiative "Businessfaktor Tax" and a regular conference leader and speaker at specialist conferences and training events.

Mr. Steef Huibregtse is the founder and CEO of TPA Global, a firm with a network in 60+ countries which runs three eco-systems: Tax, Transfer Pricing and Valuation—Tax + Technology—Global tax controversy. He has a focus on tax and technology use cases, in particularly creating turn-key solutions with "building blocks of tax technology software," i.e., workable solutions for multinationals. A whitepaper that he published on "the future of tax in 2025" does address lots of challenges and opportunities for tax professionals entering into the age of digital transformation. He is a firm believer of the "people, process & technology" approach to successfully implement such projects. He can be contacted at s.huibregtse@tpa-global.com.

Ms. Nupur Jalan is a tax professional specializing in corporate tax, international tax and transfer pricing and an interdisciplinary researcher. She can be contacted at jalannupur@outlook.com.

Jan Mendling is the Einstein-Professor of Process Science with the Department of Computer Science at Humboldt-Universität zu Berlin, Germany. His research interests include various topics in the area of business process management and information systems. He has published more than 450 research papers and articles, among others, in *Management Information Systems Quarterly, ACM Transactions on Software Engineering and Methodology, IEEE Transactions on Software Engineering, Journal of the Association of Information Systems and Decision Support Systems.* He is a department editor for Business and Information Systems Engineering, member of the board of the Austrian Society for Process Management (http://prozesse.at), one of the founders of the Berlin BPM Community of Practice (http://www.bpmb.de), organizer of several academic events on process management, and a member of the IEEE Task Force on Process Mining. He is the co-author of the textbooks *Fundamentals of Business Process Management,* Second Edition (http://fundamentals-of-bpm.org/) and Wirtschaftsinformatik, Twelfth Edition (https://lehrbuch-wirtschaftsinformatik.org/), which are extensively used in information systems education.

Dr. Robert Müller LL.M. wrote his doctoral thesis on combating VAT evasion in tax law with the help of blockchain technology. He is currently working intensively on technical and legal issues relating to the use and development of blockchain applications for taxpayers and tax administrations. He advocates for the tokenization of tax law.

Mr. Jasper Verkamman is a Junior Associate at TPA Global, a firm that specializes in coaching companies with their digital transformation projects. He is the contact person for the software solutions connected to e-Bright and TPA Global, allowing him an overview of the possibilities across the board. He can be contacted at j.verkamman @tpa-global.com.

Summary of Contents

List of Figures

List of Tables

Preface

While digitization has been advancing for a long time and has revolutionized many business sectors, the tax industry is just starting to experience the beginning of a digital transformation. TaxTech companies, as being global tax advisory firms, not only want to change the tax advisory industry at the edges, but also do not want to support the conventional work of tax folks anymore; moreover, they want to fundamentally change and revolutionize the TaxTech industry. While digital transformation has already separated the leading companies from all others in other business areas, such separation could soon be expected for the tax advisory industry. TaxTech service offerings will prevail in competition. In addition, the tax authorities are fascinated by the newly developed options to secure full transparency of tax processes. The after BEPS 1.0, initiatives were conducted into domestic tax law. Further controls and tax risk management will be the future.

Digitization is not just about software. It is also about work-flow assessment, process analysis, information flows, training, collaboration, and a paradigm shift in management. The digitization of the TaxTech industry will lead to a better integration of tax services into taxpayers' processes. So far, digital transformation in the tax industry has progressed comparatively slowly, since digitized tax services are heavily regulated, and the tax industry has managed well without the demand for digital contributions. Furthermore, the tax sector is very precedent-based; however, today's world demands more innovation than precedent. Therefore, the tax advisory industry needs to be more progressive and revitalized through digital transformation.

Today, unlike the past, technology is not demanded just for the sake of technology. The use of digital technology has become a core business need, although it is not to be expected that tax service providers, themselves, will experience an immense technological change. Rather, a paradigm shift in business and behavior is to be expected. The parties involved in TaxTech advice will change. Tax service providers will become customers of tax product providers. There will no longer be a dialog only between the service providers and their clients, but the tax product providers will also be involved in the consulting and tax administration relationship.

The phrase should be "from tax services to tax products." Hence, we have decided to dedicate the second Symposium on Digital Taxation, which was held on September 13, 2021, to the topic "Tax Law and Digitization: How to Combine Legal Tech and Tax Tech?." This book is based on the presentations held at this conference and aims to contribute to the future development of the digital tax landscape.

The editors would like to thank V,alentin Bendlinger and Hedwig Pfanner for the preparation of this book, and in particular Hedwig Pfanner for the organization of the conference. Without their dedication, the success of the conference and the completion of this book would not have been possible. The editors also wish to thank all of the contributors for their patience in revising their chapters, and Dr. Julienne Stewart-Sandgren for the linguistic editing.

Without financial support, our research would not be possible. Hence, we owe our greatest thanks to the "Jubiläumsfonds der Stadt Wien" for funding our research projects relating to the development of TaxTech.

Prof. Michael Lang
Prof. Robert Risse

CHAPTER 1

The Most Current Developments in Information Systems and the Example of Digital Platforms

Walter Brenner & Benjamin Hils

1 INTRODUCTION

1.1 Digitization of Economy and Society

The digitization of the economy and society is one of the most important developments over the past ten years. All areas of private and professional life are affected by the use of information and communication technology. We have learned that for almost every challenge we face, there is support from information and communication technology.[1] Today, if we need a flashlight, if we want to listen to music, if we want to communicate with someone, there is an application. Every reader of this chapter can draw on examples and has had their own experiences, probably both positive and negative, in dealing with information and communication technology.

Digitization is having a major impact on the corporate landscape. By comparing the ten most valuable companies in 2000, 2010 and 2020, the impact of digitization on the economy becomes clear. Table 1.1 shows the development of the world's most valuable companies from 2000 to 2020.

Table 1.1 Development of the World's Most Valuable Companies from 2000 to 2020[2]

	2000	*Mrd*	*2010*	*Mrd*	*31. März 2020*	*Mrd*
1	General Electric, USA	475	Exxon Mobil, USA	351	Saudi Arabian Oil, Saudi Arabia	1602
2	Exxon Mobil, USA	302	Petrochina, China	293	**Microsoft, USA**	1200
3	Pfizer, USA	290	**Apple, USA**	285	**Apple, USA**	1113
4	Cisco Systems, USA	269	ICBC, China	236	**Amazon, USA**	971
5	Wal Mart Stores, UK	237	China Construction Bank, China	224	**Alphabet Inc., USA**	799
6	Vodafone, USA	237	BHP Billiton, Australia	220	**Alibaba, China**	522
7	**Microsoft, USA**	231	**Microsoft, USA**	216	**Facebook, USA**	475
8	Citigroup, USA	229	China Mobile, China	202	**Tencent, China**	469
9	American Intl., USA	228	Petrobas, Brasilien	199	Berkshire Hathaway, USA	443
10	Merck & Co., USA	216	Berkshire Hathaway, USA	198	Johnson & Johnson, USA	346

Digital platforms: bold

Source: Forbes.com, Bloomberg.

1. Statistica, *Anzahl der verfügbaren Apps in den Top App-Stores im 2. Quartal 2019*, https://de.statista.com/statistik/daten/studie/208599/umfrage/anzahl-der-apps-in-den-top-app-stores/ (accessed February 2, 2022).
2. Forbes website, forbes.com (accessed February 2, 2022); Bloomberg website, bloomberg.com (accessed February 2, 2022).

In 2000 and 2010, Microsoft was one of the top ten information and communications technology companies. In 2020, seven of the ten most valuable companies in the world were digital and platform companies. This development shows the power of digitization,[3] but it also shows that none of these digital companies come from Europe. However, it is expected that not only in the USA and China, but also in Europe, digital companies and platforms will gain in importance in the future.

1.2 Digitization and Taxes

Tax consequences play a major role in the change of existing or the development of new business models and, thus, also in the digital world, even if this is not taken into account in many innovation models.[4] Failure to consider the tax consequences of business model innovations can pose an existential threat to these very developments. Companies are threatened with financial penalties in the course of tax audits, which can even lead to losses depending on the business model and margin. At the same time, errors in tax management can lead to unwanted double taxation scenarios. Last but not least, even liability issues for senior executives cannot be completely ruled out. Seldom actively mentioned but not to be neglected is the threat of loss of image as a "tax dodger." In the recent past, large international corporations, in particular, have fallen into disrepute in society on the basis of their international tax structuring models. When dealing comprehensively with the topic of "digitization and taxes," it is not only about the tax consequences of new business models, but about a whole series of aspects that are partially interrelated:

- Taxation of companies in a digital economy: new business models and new, exclusively digital products require an adjustment of the taxation of companies. If it is not possible to arrive at a globally fair taxation of the digital corporations, individual countries and economic areas will adopt their own regulations, which will make digital business more difficult to the detriment of all stakeholders.
- Digitization of tax departments in companies: using potentials of information and communication technology to automate processes that deal with taxes in companies and use tax data to manage and shape the companies.
- Digitization of tax authorities: potentials of digitization to digitize and automate tax authorities, especially processes, and to use tax data in accordance with the law.[5] The exchange of information between authorities, nationally or internationally, is an example of the use of the potentials of digitization among authorities. The use of data made available by the internet, either legally, officially or illegally by insiders, to create transparency about paid and unpaid

3. Felix Wegener, *Digitale Plattformen im e-Commerce*, Whitepaper e-Commerce & Retail, 1, (2017).
4. Deloitte, *Update: Taxation of digital business models*, https://www2.deloitte.com/de/de/pages/tax/articles/besteuerung-digitaler-geschaeftsmodelle.html (accessed February 2, 2022).
5. Official Journal of the European Union, *Council Directive 2011/16/EU*, 64 L 1 (2011), https://eur-lex.europa.eu/legal-content/EN/TXT/PDF/?uri=CELEX:32011L0016&from=DE (accessed January 1, 2022).

taxes is another effect of the digitization of the economy and society. For example, the evaluation of the so-called Panama Papers has attracted worldwide attention and triggered a discussion about the taxation of assets that are invested offshore.

With Taxtech,[6] a new field of knowledge has emerged at the interfaces between computer science, information systems,[7] and corporate taxation.[8]

1.3 Objectives of This Chapter and Methodology

This chapter cannot deal with all the developments of digitization in tax areas. It pursues three main objectives:

(1) present selected aspects of digitalization; that is, developments in information and communication technology that will have an impact on corporate tax departments in the future;
(2) present the challenges for companies using the example of the business model "digital platforms"; and
(3) present digital transformation procedures for corporate tax departments in order to make the digital transformation comprehensible and professional.

This Chapter is based on literature and internet research, as well as interviews with experts. Through this process, it became clear that the topic of "Digitization and Taxes" is still in its infancy. A documented and consolidated "state of the art" was not found. This is surprising given the great importance of taxes for the economic success of companies.

The introduction of this chapter is followed by an overview of selected development trends in digitization in section 2. This section is structured according to eight trends that will have to be taken into account in the digitization of corporate tax departments in the future. The section 3 uses digital platforms to show what challenges there are for companies and corporate tax departments in an increasingly digitized economy and what the implications are for companies. In the section 4, the authors address digital transformation. The section is divided into "Unfreezing," "Moving" and "Refreezing" according to Lewin's transformation model. Section 5 describes the impact of digitization on the corporate tax department. Section 6 contains a brief summary.

6. Handelsblatt Fachmedien, *Tax Technology Conference 2021*, https://tax-tech-conference.de/ (accessed July 13, 2021).
7. Peter Fettke, *Der TaxTech-Würfel und das TaxTech-Haus zur digitalen Transformation der Steuerfunktion*, https://www.tax-legal-excellence.com/autor/peter-fettke/ (accessed February 2, 2022).
8. Excellence Media GmbH, *Tax & Legal Excellence*, https://www.tax-legal-excellence.com/ (accessed February 2, 2022).

2 DEVELOPMENT TRENDS IN DIGITIZATION

2.1 Overview

By way of qualification, it should be said at the beginning of this section that neither practice nor science is in a position to forecast the development trends of digitization consistently, credibly, and comprehensibly in all its breadth and uncertainty. There is also no established and robust process that allows to predict the future of digitization. The reasons for this situation lie in: the breadth of digitization; the many locations and institutions working on the future; and the very different self-interests of the stakeholders.

There are numerous companies that mainly deal with forecasts on the future development of information and communication technology, such as Gartner,[9] Capgemini,[10] Handelsblatt Research,[11] or Forrester Research,[12] and also consulting and technology companies[13] and scientists who have dealt with the development lines of digitization for the economy and society or for sub-areas, such as the digitization of the corporate tax department.[14]

For this Chapter, we have drawn on publicly available information from companies such as Gartner, from consulting firms, and work from academia. We have consolidated these individual contributions through interviews with experts. The authors of this Chapter make no claim to the completeness or general validity of their view of the future. They have compiled and prioritized the information available to them. They are aware that other experts, even if they had the same information, could arrive at different lines of development for digitization.

From the authors' perspective, the following eight trends can be identified for digitization:

(1) the performance of hardware, software, and networks will continue to increase as prices tend to fall;
(2) services from the cloud will gain in importance;

9. Gartner website, https://www.gartner.com/en (accessed February 2, 2022).
10. Capgemini, *Studie IT-Trends 2021: Neuausrichtung und Pläne für das New Normal*, https://www.capgemini.com/de-de/2021/04/digitalisierung-it-trends-budget/ (accessed February 2, 2022).
11. Handelsblatt Research Institute, *Trendradar TAX*, https://research.handelsblatt.com/assets/uploads/Trendradar%20Tax.pdf#wt_eid=2162514664600976202&wt_t=1626073489215 (accessed February 2, 2022).
12. Forrester website, https://go.forrester.com/ (accessed July 12).
13. IBM Research, *Science & Technology Outlook 2021*, IBM Corporation Whitepaper (2021); Kevin Sneader & Shubham Singhal, *The next normal arrives: Trends that will define 2021—and beyond*, https://www.mckinsey.com/featured-insights/leadership/the-next-normal-arrives-trends-that-will-define-2021-and-beyond (accessed February 2, 2022).
14. EY, *Tax technology and data*, https://www.ey.com/en_gl/tax/technology-data (accessed February 2, 2022); Fritz Esterer & Christian Baumgart, *Digitalisierung von Steuerabteilungen*, Aktuelle Entwicklungen im Wirtschafts- und Steuerrecht 39, (2020); KPMG, *Tax Technology*, https://home.kpmg/de/de/home/dienstleistungen/tax-legal/tax-technology.html (accessed February 2, 2022); PWC, *Tax Technology & Data Analytics*, https://www.pwc.ch/en/services/tax-advice/tax-technology.html (accessed February 2, 2022).

(3) the amount of digital data will increase;
(4) computer-based capabilities for analyzing data will increase;
(5) automation and real-time processing of processes will increase;
(6) human-centeredness becomes an essential criterion;
(7) attacks on digital processing will increase; and
(8) new business models, especially digital platforms, will prevail.

In the following Sections, the authors describe each of these eight trends and briefly address what the trends mean for the corporate tax department.

2.2 The Performance of Hardware, Software, and Networks Will Continue to Increase as Prices Tend to Fall

The continuous, sometimes even erratic, development of information and communication technology has been, is and will continue to be, the central driver of digitization. The central guiding principle for digitization is Moore's Law,[15] named after Gordon B. Moore, one of the founders of Intel. He describes that the capacity of processors doubles every eighteen months at roughly the same cost. However, there are always discussions about when Moore's law will no longer apply. To date, there is no evidence that the development of information and communication technology will not continue at least at the same rate as in the past. The falling cost of processors while performance remains the same, a relationship that can also be derived from Moore's law, has led to a steady increase in the penetration of digital devices into the economy and society.

Hardware performance will continue to increase over the next few years, at least at the same rate as in the past.[16] This means that, on the one hand, it will be increasingly possible to perform even complex processing on small devices and, on the other hand, that almost infinite processing capacities will be available in the data centers of the future, and this at prices that are tending to fall. The miniaturization of processors will increase, and energy consumption will decrease. Hence, these two developments will increase the use of hardware. With so-called quantum computing,[17] a new generation of processors is available whose performance is dramatically greater than that of processors available today. In 2021, quantum computers were only at the beginning of their use in the military, public administrations, and companies. However, it is expected that they will find their way into more and more companies in the coming years, opening up new dimensions of processing. The increase in hardware performance also applies to memory. They are becoming smaller and smaller as prices tend to fall, and memory density is increasing. In the future, this will make it possible

15. Intel, *Über 50 Jahre Mooresches Gesetz,* https://www.intel.de/content/www/de/de/silicon-innovations/moores-law-technology.html (accessed February 2, 2022).
16. Kristin Rinortner, *Warum das Mooresche Gesetz nicht tot ist,* https://www.datacenter-insider.de/warum-das-mooresche-gesetz-nicht-tot-ist-a-967973/ (accessed February 2, 2022).
17. Kasey Panetta, Gartner Insights, https://www.gartner.com/smarterwithgartner/the-cios-guide-to-quantum-computing (accessed January 1, 2022).

to store data almost indefinitely, regardless of the format. Subsequently, this development will improve the processing of image, voice, and video data.

The performance of software will increase in the next few years in the same way as hardware. The further development of software will be characterized by new possibilities of programming, such as agile programming, but also by improved possibilities for non-informaticians to write software (low code).[18] In addition, there will be a software solution for almost every challenge in private and business life in the future. The spectrum ranges from software that turns a smartphone into a flashlight, to complex software for business management control of systems and production control software for large companies, to real-time systems for military purposes or for controlling autonomous vehicles. From a business perspective, it will be a generation of ERP systems, newly called "Digital Core," that will encompass almost all business management processes. SAP S/4 HANA[19] is a prominent example of software for the "Digital Core." In addition, there will still be new dedicated software for individual areas of a company, such as the corporate tax department. Open source will become more important in the coming years. It is to be expected that large companies will make parts of their software landscape available to other companies as open source with the idea that they will further develop the software and in turn share it.

The capacity and availability of networks will also continue to increase.[20] This applies to both wired networks and networks that transmit data over the air. The penetration of fiber optic cables will continue to increase in the sense of fiber optic cabling into private homes. The change in mobile networks from 4G to 5G will increase the performance of radio networks and of great importance for new uses of the new radio networks, in the field of mobility, is the reduction of the latency. Latency stands for the time between the sending of a signal and the response to this signal. Very often, latency is equated with the response time of an information system. Further development steps are also underway in the area of satellite communication in order to have sufficient bandwidth available for digital communication everywhere in the world.

Significance for the corporate tax department is the monetary investment hurdle in tax technology; that is, cost of new technologies and tools, are continuously decreasing, while the benefits are increasing. It is possible to store data on a large scale and perform processing that was unthinkable just a few years ago. The corporate tax department has to deal with this massive shift in "processing boundaries." In addition, solutions for the corporate tax department are becoming an integrated part of many ERP systems. Established stand-alone solutions and tools, such as Excel can be replaced at much better rates.

---

18. Gartner, *Gartner Glossary: Information Technology Glossary: Citizen Developer*, https://www.gartner.com/en/information-technology/glossary/citizen-developer (accessed February 2, 20 22); Gartner peer insights, *Enterprise Low-Code Application Platforms (LCAP) Reviews and Ratings*, https://www.gartner.com/reviews/market/enterprise-low-code-application-platform (accessed February 2, 2022).
19. SAP, *Was ist SAP S/4HANA?*, https://www.sap.com/swiss/products/s4hana-erp.html (accessed February 2, 2022).
20. Ferry Grijpink et al., Connected World: An evolution in connectivity beyond the 5G revolution, McKinsey Global Institute 1, (2020).

2.3 Services from the Cloud Will Gain in Importance

The developments in hardware, software and networks described above have led to the emergence of centralized, globally available data centers from which various services can be obtained. They form the basis of digital platforms, which in some cases connect billions of providers and customers with each other for business purposes. The spectrum ranges from infrastructure services, such as processing or storage capacity, to highly specialized, dedicated applications or the app world, which is available on smartphones, for example. The internet giants in particular, such as Amazon, Apple, Facebook, Google and Microsoft, each own numerous data centers distributed around the world from which they offer services. The internet giants dominate the world of cloud and dictate services, quality, and prices to their customers. The importance of the cloud for information processing in the coming years will continue to grow rapidly.[21] Despite these objections to the dominance of the internet giants in the cloud, many innovative applications used by many companies, for example, for the analysis of large data sets, and private individuals, are not possible without the use of the cloud.

Many European and especially German-speaking companies still have major concerns about outsourcing parts of their digital infrastructure or applications to the cloud. The explanations are manifold: legal aspects, data protection, confidentiality, and availability are some of the concerns that are repeatedly cited. Against this background, it can also be explained that dealing with the cloud is still an open question in many companies. From the point of view of the authors of this Chapter, the importance of the cloud will continue to increase in the coming years. This is also reflected in the "TrendradarCIO," which is compiled by the Institute of Information Systems at the University of St. Gallen.[22] The proportion of applications that are moved to the cloud or obtained from the cloud will increase. In the area of data analytics or the use of artificial intelligence, it is already no longer possible for many companies without using services from the cloud. In the future, numerous companies will obtain SAP S/4 Hana from the cloud; for example, from Amazon. The availability and security of cloud-based offerings are generally higher than that of solutions operated by medium-sized companies in particular.

Significance for the corporate tax department: increasingly, sensitive company data is no longer physically stored in the filing cabinet, instead, digitally outside the company in the cloud. The corporate tax department must define its requirements for data protection, confidentiality, and data security. In addition, the impact of new data

21. Gartner, *Gartner identifiziert die wichtigsten strategischen Technologietrends für 2021*, https://www.gartner.de/de/newsroom/pressemitteilungen/2020-10-19-gartner-identifiziert-die-wichtigsten-strategischen-technologietrends-fuer-2021(accessed February 2, 2022).
22. Walter Brenner, Rolf Trüeb & Barbara Brenner, *TrendradarCIO 2021-2 – CIO Roundtable: Die IT befindet sich auf dem Weg zurück in die (neue) «Normalität»*, https://media-exp1.licdn.com/dms/document/C4D1FAQG4gRAoceQ2Fw/feedshare-document-pdf-analyzed/0/1627904115817?e=1630443600&v=beta&t=A0alJLIU1Mzy-X8NVt8ZWX40c7B8Wc_5-xGL-afd1TM (accessed February 2, 2022).

protection regulations must be examined, and the requirements implemented. Employees in corporate tax departments must, therefore, also build up a solid knowledge in adjacent areas of law.

2.4 The Amount of Digital Data Will Increase

The development trends of digitization already described have led to growth in data. This growth will continue.[23] The basic hypothesis is: the more digital devices are used, the more data will be available. “Big Data,”[24] the identifier for this development direction of digitization, stands for the ability of companies to deal with huge amounts of data. Four development directions, the four Vs, characterize “Big Data”: Volume stands for the large amount of data; Velocity for the speed at which the data is generated; Variety for the different formats in which the data is generated, and Veracity for the authenticity of the data.

The growth of data, as already described, is due to the number of devices that generate data, combined with the possibility of transferring this data to the cloud via the internet. The aviation industry provides good examples of large amounts of data generated by sensors; for example, on the Airbus A 350 model 6000 sensors are said to collect every day about 2.5 Terabytes data.[25] Another important driver of the growth in data is the ability to store not only formatted data or text, but also large quantities of images, speech, and videos, even in high quality.

The growth of data takes place, on the one hand, within the company, on the other hand, also outside the company on the internet.[26] When talking about the growing importance of data as a resource for companies today, the data available on the internet must also be included in the consideration. Some of the data on the internet is available free of charge, while others are subject to a fee. For example, weather data of varying quality can be obtained from the internet at very different prices. Linking internal and external data can greatly improve the results when evaluating data.

The quality of data available for analysis is constantly growing. Nevertheless, not all data, supplied by sensors or obtained from the internet today, are at a satisfactory quality level so that they are valuable for analyses. Partly, dedicated software is necessary to check and ensure the quality of the data.[27]

---

23. Statistica, *Volume of data/information created, captured, copied, and consumed worldwide from 2010 to 2025*, https://www.statista.com/statistics/871513/worldwide-data-created/#:~:text=The%20total%20amount%20of%20data,replicated%20reached%20a%20new%20high (accessed February 2, 2022).
24. Oracle, *What is Big Data?*, https://www.oracle.com/big-data/what-is-big-data/ (accessed February 2, 2022).
25. Walter Schadhauser & Rainer Graefen, *Wo kommen all die Daten her?*, https://www.storage-insider.de/wo-kommen-all-die-daten-her-a-608824/ (accessed February 2, 2022).
26. Max Roser, Hannah Ritchie & Esteban Ortiz-Ospina, *Internet*, https://ourworldindata.org/internet (accessed February 2, 2022); Statistica, *Volume of data/information created, captured, copied, and consumed worldwide from 2010 to 2025*, https://www.statista.com/statistics/871513/worldwide-data-created/ (accessed February 2, 2022).
27. Boris Otto & Hubert Österle, *Corporate Data Quality: Voraussetzung erfolgreicher Geschäftsmodelle* (Gabler Verlag 2016).

Data analytics[28] stands for the analysis of digital data sets. In recent years, data analytics has emerged as a new important task in companies. The central goal of data analytics is to recognize structures and correlations in large data sets and to derive forecasts or recognize anomalies from them. In more and more companies, data-driven management is establishing a paradigm in which estimates or hunches are replaced by data and its evaluation. Relatively, it should be noted that correlation measured by analysis of data should not be confused with causality.

The growth of data leads to a new transparency of information that is accessible through the internet, which has been unknown in history until now. This democratization of knowledge leads, on the one hand, to the fact that the concealment of information, in order to exercise power through information asymmetries, loses importance and, on the other hand, that statements by experts are increasingly questioned. Extremes are the many false reports (fake news) that are deliberately put on the internet to advertise partly pointless products or services, and conversely to deliberately manipulate people. For example, within companies, transparency can be created about the real course of processes. "Process mining" as a new discipline in companies,[29] consulting and science uses data from information systems to find out how processes really run, in order to identify potential for improvement.

Significance for the corporate tax department: without the use of technological means, it will not be possible to comprehensively, store and monitor the relevant tax data. In addition, external data sets need to be quickly captured, imported into existing systems and the impact on the business assessed. The importance of comprehensive data management is increasing. Data quality in the corporate tax department is gaining importance. In addition, a data catalog should be created that provides information on what data is available in the company and in what quality. Moreover, the importance of external data is increasing.

2.5 Computer-Based Capabilities for Analyzing Data Will Increase

The growth of data, as described in section 2.4, combined with the increase in the power of processors and memory, as explained in section 2.1, has led to great improvements in algorithms for analyzing data in recent years. Data analytics has become a new discipline in business[30] and science.[31]

28. Foster Provost & Tom Fawcett, *Data Science für Unternehmen: Data Mining und datenanalytisches Denken praktisch anwenden* (mitp 2017).
29. Marlon Dumas, Marcello La Rosa & Jan Mendling, *Grundlagen des Geschäftsprozessmanagements* (Springer Verlag GmbH 2021); Wil M. P. van der Aalst, *Process Mining: Data Science in Action* (Springer Verlag GmbH 2016).
30. Christian Dremel, Matthias M. Herterich, Jochen Wulf, Jean-Claude Waizmann & Walter Brenner, *How AUDI AG Established Big Data Analytics in Its Digital Transformation*, 16(2) MIS Quarterly Executive 81 (2017).
31. Filip Fatz, Philip Hake & Peter Fettke, *Towards Tax Compliance by Design: A Decentralized Validation of Tax Processes Using Blockchain Technology*, Conference on Business Informatics (2019); Galit Shmueli & Otto R. Koppius, *Predictive Analytics in Information Systems Research*, 35(3) Mis Quarterly 553 (2011).

The analysis of data using statistical programs, such as SPSS, has been around for many decades. Samples, which were usually representative, were often evaluated and conclusions were drawn about the population, and hypotheses were tested and verified or falsified. There are three main directions for increasing the ability to analyze data: (1) Direction 1 means that the evaluation is no longer based on randomly collected data, but on all available data that is measured or collected on the internet, for example, changes in the sales behavior of customers on Amazon by analyzing all sales transactions,[32] (2) Direction 2 is based on the fact that the number of variables that can be taken into account for evaluations can be increased. In particular, external data can also be included in the evaluations, and (3) Direction 3 concerns algorithms. Through the use of artificial intelligence methods, new evaluation possibilities are available that are able to recognize correlations, structures, and anomalies in data. For the last two to three years, it has been common practice in the press, in companies, and also in science to present the use of artificial intelligence methods, in particular, neural networks and unsupervised learning, as a means of solving all problems.[33] The internet giants serve as shining examples of how to use artificial intelligence. The authors do not subscribe to this euphoric sentiment. Their experience in dealing with artificial intelligence methods shows that substantial experience is still needed and that it is a laborious learning process for companies to use artificial intelligence in such a way that sustainable business success can be achieved. Despite this relativizing statement, on the use of artificial intelligence, the ability of companies to use computer-aided data analysis will increase significantly in the coming years.

Significance for the corporate tax department: data analytics allows the rapid detection of anomalies and, thus, sources of tax errors. The same applies to the tax authorities, so that an increasing transparency of business activities can be expected. This internal corporate transparency is further enhanced by the democratization of knowledge through the internet. By increasing the amount of data analyzed, by including external data and by increasing the variables to be audited, former sampling methods will be replaced by reliable and holistic results. Corporate tax departments need to build capabilities to analyze data at a high level in order to better perform operational processes so as to have fewer problems with tax authorities in the future. In addition, financial planning reliability increases because the tax consequences are clarified more quickly and precisely. Furthermore, employees in the corporate tax departments need the ability to use the technical possibilities.

32. Brent Smith & Greg Linden, *Two Decades of Recommender Systems at Amazon.com*, 21(3) IEEE Internet Computing 12, 13 (2017).
33. Walter Brenner, Benjamin van Giffen, Jana Koehler, Tobias Fahse & André Sagodi, *Bausteine eines Managements Künstlicher Intelligenz: Eine Standortbestimmung* (Springer Verlag GmbH 2021).

2.6 Automation and Real-Time Processing of Processes Will Increase

The automation of operational processes has been a central motivation since the use of information and communication technology in companies, which began in the 1960s. Time and again, over the last decades, the potential for automation seemed to be exhausted. New possibilities of information and communication technology have been created and will continue to create new possibilities for automation in the future. Four examples may support this prognosis: new integrated operational software; the use of robotic process automation; the use of chatbots; programming in specialist areas.

The core business software in companies is being further developed regularly. On the one hand, continuous improvements in the form of new versions are constantly taking place, and on the other hand, the software is being completely reprogrammed, albeit in larger periods of time. Both developments will be seen within the next few years. Currently, companies are in the process of switching their software from SAP to SAP S/4 HANA. This change, which is putting great strain on companies, offers new opportunities for automating processes. Even complicated analyses can be done almost in real time. With the introduction of this software, companies have a new "digital core" that increases the degree of automation and supports data-oriented business management through the possibilities for data analytics. In addition to the complete SAP S/4 HANA solution for all areas of the company, there will be stand-alone solutions for individual areas, such as the corporate tax department.

With Robot Process Automation,[34] a new possibility has emerged in recent years to automate processes relatively quickly. Robot Process Automation makes it possible, for example, to digitally reproduce actions performed in Word or Excel, or requiring access to a transaction system. If a process needs to be automated quickly and unspectacularly, Robot Process Automation is the right tool. Robot Process Automation has become widespread in recent years in the financial sector, among others and it is to be expected that this automation approach will continue to spread.

Chatbots[35] are software that understands speech or text, and also responds with speech or text. It has established itself in recent years as an easy way to answer recurring questions from customers quickly and cheaply. The basis of chatbots is the software's improved ability to understand speech. Over the next few years, the software's ability to understand complicated issues will improve, opening up more areas of use for chatbots. The success of voice-based speakers, such as Amazon's Alexa or the spread of Apple's Siri, show that customers are willing to communicate linguistically with computers if the user interface is easy to use and also creates directly perceivable benefits.

Another way of automating processes is the constantly improving possibilities for people in companies who have not had professional training in computer science to

34. Wil M. P. van der Aalst, Martin Bichler & Armin Heinzl, *Robotic Process Automation*, 60 Business & Information Systems Engineering 269 (2018).
35. Chatbot Research website, https://chatbotresearch.org/ (accessed February 2, 2022); Matthias Simon Billert, Tim Weinert, Andreas Janson & Jan Marco Leimeister, *Co-Creation durch Peers im digitalen Lernen – Wie Plattformen und Chatbots die Partizipation bei der Lernmaterialerstellung begleiten können*, 57 HMD Praxis der Wirtschaftsinformatik 722 (2020).

program independently. These approaches, known as "Low Code—No Code" or "Citizen Development," are becoming increasingly widespread in companies. Whether and to what extent these possibilities will become established in the next few years remains to be seen.

Significance for the corporate tax department: process analyses, process mining, and the identification of automation potentials are becoming the "normal" business of the corporate tax departments. Routine activities are being automated with the corresponding consequences for employees. In addition, tax-relevant framework conditions are changing and must be evaluated for tax consequences at the same time. Real-time adjustments to avoid negative tax effects are possible and necessary. Further, the pressure on employees to work on their qualifications is increasing.

2.7 Human-Centeredness Becomes an Essential Criterion

Larry Leifer,[36] Professor of Engineering at Stanford University in Palo Alto, coined the phrase "innovation is made by people for people." This guiding principle of design thinking[37] can be applied to digitization. If people do not understand or embrace digitization, in whatever field, it will ultimately fail. Companies like Amazon, Apple, Facebook, or Google have masterfully managed to create ecosystems that are appreciated by people all over the world and used billions of times every day. Human-centeredness in various forms has had a great impact on the success of internet giants. Design thinking is based, among other things, on the fact that it successfully combines the criteria of "feasibility," "economic viability," and "desirability" in the development of new solutions. In particular, the criterion of "desirability" is brought to the fore by design thinking, which uses special methods to identify the obvious and the hidden needs of users or customers, and to make them an integral part of innovative solutions.

The user interface will become increasingly important in the future. It will become a decisive criterion for success in the digital world. Applications that are not immediately understood will be rejected. A great deal is being invested in the graphic design of the user interface and the use of new input options, such as speech or gestures. Traditional criteria, such as availability and response time (latency), are often forgotten. Applications whose response time is too high from the user's point of view, or which are not perceived to be available constantly; that is, 24/7, are met with great disapproval by users. Correspondingly large investments in data centers and networks are necessary to optimize response times and availability.

The design of the "work of the future" will play a major role in the post-pandemic period. The pandemic, as bad as it was for the economy and society, has taught the economy and society that, among other things, working from a home office is technically possible more or less without problems and is also desired by many people.

---

36. Stanford Profiles, *Larry John Leifer*, https://profiles.stanford.edu/larry-leifer (accessed February 2, 2022).
37. IDEO Design Thinking, *Design Thinking Defined*, https://designthinking.ideo.com/ (accessed February 2, 2022); Walter Brenner & Falk Uebernickel, *Design Thinking: The Handbook* (World Scientific Publishing 2020).

Digitization has contributed significantly to the fact that the economy and society have not come to a complete standstill, instead, economic and social life has continued, even if individual sectors have suffered greatly. From the point of view of digitization, human-centeredness in "work of the future" means enabling the conditions for location-independent work at any time. This means that when working from the home office, as many processes as possible are digitized, the infrastructural prerequisites are created, and the security of processing is also guaranteed.

Ethical and moral aspects, in the context of digitization, did not play a major role in the past. A broader public became aware of this topic through discussions initiated by autonomous vehicles. At the Massachusetts Institute of Technology, a group of researchers conducted an experiment with the "Moral Machine"[38] in which they confronted the test subjects with delicate moral and ethical questions. As a result of these discussions, the German government has set up a panel of experts to create rules for dealing with autonomous vehicles. Further ethical and moral discussions have arisen around the use of artificial intelligence in companies. Surveys conducted by the authors of this Chapter, among others, show that there is also fear about the use of artificial intelligence in technology companies. The discussions about the use of facial recognition software can be cited as one example. Against this background, it is not surprising that there are calls from various interest groups for governmental or supranational regulation. It is to be expected that these discussions will continue in the coming years and will have a major influence on the further development of digitization.

Significance for the corporate tax department: the competence profile is changing from a pure legal expert to an expert for business, IT, and law. Interfaces and dashboards must be adapted to the requirements of tax experts for all complex tax compliance management functions. The increasing cockpit function, in the corporate tax department, increases the responsibility of each employee with regard to compliance and ethics. The issue of whistle-blower protection is making its way into corporate tax departments. Human-centered methods, such as design thinking, must be known, training must be available for them, and the new methods must be used.

2.8 Attacks on Digital Processing Will Increase

The number of cyberattacks on companies has risen sharply in recent years, especially during the pandemic.[39] The number of attacks varies widely and the available statistics assume a significant growth. It is only in recent days that many companies and public institutions, such as Technical University Berlin, are becoming more aware of the vulnerability of their applications and infrastructures. Only a few companies go public with reliable and concrete information about the number, impact, and severity of cyberattacks. The number of unreported cases of how many attacks there have really been and how great the damage is likely to be very large. There is a veritable "industry"

38. Moral Machine website, https://www.moralmachine.net/ (accessed February 2, 2022).
39. Purplesec, *2021 Cyber Security Statistics The Ultimate List Of Stats, Data & Trends*, https://purplesec.us/resources/cyber-security-statistics/ (accessed February 2, 2022).

for cyberattacks. Cyberattacks can even be ordered on the internet. State intelligence services and the department of defenses are, therefore, building up massive expertise in combating cyberattacks.

There is a growing awareness of the vulnerability of companies to cyberattacks because of the behavior and attitude of many users and digital customers. Two-way authorization, for example, has still little approval from many customers when it is required for electronic shopping. Investments in IT security will rise sharply in the coming years.[40] The more digitized companies there are and the more they depend on digitization, the more money and personnel they will have to invest in IT security.

Significance for the corporate tax department: the corporate tax department must be fully integrated into the company's cybersecurity strategy. "Dry runs" should be conducted showing what can happen in the event of a successful cyberattack on the corporate tax department. Awareness of cyberattack threats needs to be raised.

2.9 New Business Models, Especially Digital Platforms, Will Prevail

A business model determines the way a company or business unit functions to generate profit. In order to work a business model, numerous aspects of a company have to be designed. The Business Model Canvas by Pigneur and Osterwalder[41] shows essential aspects to consider when thinking about changing existing business models or creating new ones. Gassmann[42] has investigated what types of business models there are and has come across 55. The study of new business models is fascinating and founders in particular like to take their cue from "lighthouse figures" from Silicon Valley.

Digitization has enabled numerous new business models. Many companies have grown strongly as a result of these new business models. Enormous company values have been created, as we have already presented in section 1 and as the ranking of the most valuable companies, in 2018, as shown in Table 1.1, section 1.

The emergence of new business models is one of the central and most far-reaching effects of digitization. The effects on the future structures of the economy and society are not yet foreseeable today. However, they are likely to be greater than is currently expected. Digital platforms will be of great importance in the future. Section 3 of this Chapter will, therefore, discuss the potential of digital platforms and outline the impact that the operation of digital platforms will have on the corporate tax departments of companies.

The pandemic, especially the retail lockdown, drastically demonstrated to many companies that digital business models, such as selling through the internet, are not a "nice to have" but a "must have" option. Businesses that were unable to digitally

40. Statistica, *Ausgaben für IT-Sicherheit weltweit im Jahr 2020 nach Marktsegment und Prognose für 2021*, https://de.statista.com/statistik/daten/studie/151720/umfrage/it-sicherheitsumsatz-nach-marktsegmenten-weltweit/#: ~ :text = Die%20weltweiten%20Ausgaben%20f%C3%BCr%20IT,5%20Milliarden%20US%2DDollar%20prognostiziert (accessed February 2, 2022).
41. Alexander Osterwalder & Yves Pigneur, *Business Model Generation: A Handbook for Visionaries, Game Changers, and Challengers* (John Wiley & Sons 2010).
42. Oliver Gassmann, Karolin Frankenberger & Michaela Csik, *Geschäftsmodelle entwickeln: 55 innovative Konzepte mit dem St. Galler Business Model Navigator* (Cark Hanser Verlag 2013).

interact with customers were simply "out of business" during the pandemic. It is to be expected that as a late consequence of the pandemic, the transformation of existing, primarily physical, business models into digital business models will take place.

Digital service providers are emerging for many tasks and challenges of the economy and society. Some of these only take on individual tasks at the beginning, but gradually increase their range of services. For example, the digital service provider taxdoo.com was created to digitize and automate the payment of sales tax in e-commerce.[43]

Significance for the corporate tax department: the corporate tax department must be involved in new business activities considerably and at an early stage. Taxes are becoming a success and business factor for companies. The corporate tax department is advancing from a service department to an active co-designer and driver for business. Corporate tax departments need to build up knowledge about innovative business models and their tax implications. The corporate tax department tends to become an exchange platform for internal and external data exchange. In addition, the corporate tax department is increasingly becoming an internal and external communication interface. In the past, the corporate tax department only communicated with the tax authorities and the tax consultancy. In the future, the corporate tax department will be in contact with all business partners.

3 DIGITAL PLATFORMS

In this Section, the challenges for fair taxation in an increasingly digitalized economy and the requirements for the digitization of the corporate tax department are discussed using the example of digital platforms. The authors have chosen digital platforms as an application example because of their great economic importance.

3.1 Linear Business Models Versus Digital Platform

The majority of companies are based on classic, so-called linear business models. In this type of business model, value is created step by step. The process runs in a straight line, starting with the suppliers, through manufacturing to logistics and the final sale to the end customer. The entire value chain must be controlled and managed by companies for each product.[44] With linear business models, the advantage is that processes can be continuously tested and efficiently set up. The agility of business processes is low. Business partners, customers, and markets are known and efforts to comply with regulations of a legal and ethical nature can be minimized. These advantages are offset by new requirements and reporting obligations. Among other things, non-financial reporting is catching up with financial reporting. A recently

43. Taxdoo website, https://www.taxdoo.com/ (accessed February 2, 2022).
44. Harald Pöttinger, *Was zeichnet ein Plattform-Geschäftsmodell aus?*, http://haraldpoettinger.com/plattform-geschaeftsmodell/ (accessed February 2, 2022).

published proposal to amend the CSR Directive, for example, the Corporate Sustainability Reporting Directive, requires this effective from 2023.[45] Long process chains with many participants will thus become a challenge for companies. Purely economically driven business models, which are only geared towards profit targets, must be checked for the aspect of sustainability. The administrative reporting effort increases in any case. Moreover, adjustments in the value chain based on non-financial aspects cannot be ruled out.

As already explained at the beginning of this Chapter, platforms represent the business model basis for the now most successful and valuable companies worldwide. The digitization push of recent years has enabled the leap to the next evolutionary stage of marketplaces. Digital platforms enable new value creation models for companies. Well-known examples of digital platforms are Amazon, Apple, Facebook, Google, Netflix, Uber.[46] The first successful models are emerging in Europe and Germany as well, such as XOM Materials, initiated by Klöckner & Co. and aim to become the Amazon of the steel industry.[47] This trend is fundamentally increasing. In 2014, while 81 digital platforms were represented in the economic sector in Germany, Austria, and Switzerland, this number almost doubled to 173 digital platforms by 2020.[48]

The advantages of digital platforms are that they generate added value by bringing together and connecting customers, manufacturers, and providers, so-called ecosystem partners, for example. This facilitates automated interactions and transactions in a multi-sided model to create a network effect. Each actor can play one or more roles in each scenario.

Digital platforms, therefore, create new potentials for platform operators and platform partners.[49] The *network effect is* considered the starting point for successful platform models. This is generally understood to be an effect in which the benefit of a product increases with the number of users and so-called positive network effects arise. Such effects occur in particular with internet platforms, for example, with auction houses or contact forums. If the number of suppliers and consumers on a platform increases, a connection effect automatically arises. The combination of supply and demand is optimized on the platform. Concentrating on one platform increases transparency in terms of quality and price, so that suppliers and consumers can make better decisions and derive additional benefits from an increased information base. The authors refer to this as the so-called positive transparency effect. Thanks to modern technologies, the increasing number of users and transactions enables the collection of qualified data sets. This data effect supports the international merging of supply and

45. PWC, *CSR-Richtlinie: Heute beginnt eine neue Ära in der Nachhaltigkeitsberichterstattung. Was zeichnet ein Plattform-Geschäftsmodell aus?*, https://www.pwc.de/de/pressemitteilungen/2021/csr-richtlinie-heute-beginnt-eine-neue-aera-in-der-nachhaltigkeitsberichterstattung.html (accessed February 2, 2022).
46. Jürgen Mauerer, *Der Netzwerkeffekt bringt den Erfolg*, https://www.com-magazin.de/praxis/business-it/netzwerkeffekt-bringt-erfolg-2558269.html (accessed February 2, 2022).
47. EY Etventure, *Klöckner vs. Stahlindustrie*, etventure GmbH Whitepaper.
48. Susan Rönisch, *Übersicht: Zahl der Online-Marktplätze im DACH-Raum explodiert*, https://www.onetoone.de/artikel/db/129304SUR.html (accessed February 2, 2022).
49. Harald Pöttinger, *Netzwerkeffekte befeuern das Geschäftsmodell der Plattform*, http://haraldpoettinger.com/plattform-netzwerkeffekte/ (accessed February 2, 2022).

demand and provides information for the continuous optimization of the platforms. In addition, modern possibilities of data analysis provide the opportunity to evaluate large sets of data, so these must be included as a significant value driver in the evaluation of platform models. Digital platforms soften trade and national borders and unleash themselves from the chains of stationary marketplaces. Market participants can interact with players all over the world without a physical presence. This internationalization effect is reinforced when purely digital goods or services are exchanged on digital platforms, as these can be multiplied and distributed according to their definition and characteristics, at low additional variable costs.[50]

3.2 Challenges for States and Companies

From a technical point of view, the emergence of digital platforms is "only" an evolutionary step. It is disruptive in many industries and of the highest economic importance at the same time. The great economic potential of digital platforms has created a need for action on the part of policymakers. New framework conditions must be created that promote the establishment of and participation in platform models. A revision and adaptation of international legal regulations are important in order to ensure a correct distribution of value creation and fair competition. The BMWi in Germany explicitly names three cornerstones that must be observed:[51] (1) data and data sovereignty, (2) competition and market power, and (3) telecommunications law.

The authors add a fourth point to these aspects. In the ongoing discussions, the taxation of digital business models, and thus, digital platforms should play a weighty role. For a country, taxes are, by definition, sources of revenue for financing the state budget. For companies, taxes have long since become a business factor, as positive margins in strong competitive environments are often only possible through perfect revenue and cost optimization. This has a direct impact on business locations that are seldom considered in the debate. After-tax return is a key metric for investment decision makers. Decision makers weigh and rank their investment targets with regard to the expected return.[52] High tax rates and complex legal structures reduce margins, increase risks, and consequently reduce the attractiveness of locations for investors and companies. The taxation of digital business models, their products, and players must, therefore, be clearly regulated, internationally competitive, and easy for companies to manage.

50. Nils Urbach, *Betriebswirtschaftliche Besonderheiten digitaler Güter*, https://www.fim-rc.de/Paperbibliothek/Veroeffentlicht/588/wi-588.pdf (accessed February 2, 2022).
51. Bundesministerium für Wirtschaft und Energie, *Digitale Plattformen*, https://www.bmwi.de/Redaktion/DE/Artikel/Digitale-Welt/digitale-plattformen.html (accessed February 2, 2022).
52. Bert Rürup & Alex Schrinner, *Neustart mit Altlasten*, https://www.handelsblatt.com/adv/tax-initiative/analyse-neustart-mit-altlasten/27057586.html (accessed February 2, 2022).

3.3 International Tax Policy

When considering the current international recommendations, guidelines, and directives on the taxation of digital business models, it is up to the individual countries to transpose these regulations into national law. Even if the harmonization of international tax regulations has strived for years, national differences in tax laws are the rule. The implementation of the OECD's BEPS (Base Erosion and Profit Shifting) project is a good example. Although guidelines have been issued by the EU for the member states, the detailed implementation is still left to the individual countries.[53] As a result, companies must monitor all regulations per country in which they are economically active and follow the rules applicable there. In the framework of the EU-DAC-6 Directive, all member states were recently obliged to report cross-border tax arrangements. As a result, the documentation requirements for the corporate tax departments are increasing immensely.[54]

Back in 2015, the OECD published a final report with a total of fifteen action points as part of the BEPS project. These action points were aimed at undesirable profit reduction and relocation by multinational companies.[55] The first action point, "Addressing the Tax Challenges of the Digital Economy," was dedicated to the increasingly digitized economy and also purely digital business models with the awareness that the existing tax systems could not take sufficient account of the new business models to avoid profit shifting and shortcuts in the long term. The overarching objective of this OECD project was to ensure that taxation occurs at the place of entrepreneurial activity and economic value creation.[56] On July 1, 2021, a revolutionary evolution of the OECD Guidelines transpired. Through the drive of the G20 countries, the OECD developed a two-pillar plan and launched a fundamental reform of international corporate taxation. As of July 5, 2021, 131 countries have already agreed to fair distribution rights and a uniform minimum tax rate of at least 15%.[57] The first pillar is intended to guarantee the stability of the international tax system and ensure a coordinated, fair distribution of tax revenues. Thus, individual courses of action and legislation by individual countries are to be prevented, which would certainly promote further tax structuring incentives for companies and tax revenue losses for the states. Pillar 2 regulates the global effective minimum taxation. Both pillars will technically be developed by Q4 2021 and

53. Bundesministerium für Finanzen, *Überblick über das BEPS-Projekt von OECD und G20*, https://www.bundesfinanzministerium.de/Content/DE/Standardartikel/Themen/Steuern/2017-06-07-beps-gewinnkuerzung-und-gewinnverlagerung.html (accessed February 2, 2022).
54. Bakertilly, *Meldepflichten für grenzüberschreitende Steuergestaltungen ("DAC 6")*, https://www.bakertilly.de/services/baker-tilly-digital/alle-baker-tilly-digital-services/dac-6.html (accessed February 2, 2022).
55. OECD, *Inclusive Framework on Base Erosion and Profit Shifting (BEPS)*, https://www.oecd.org/tax/beps/beps-actions/ (accessed January 1, 2022)
56. Bundesministerium für Finanzen, *Überblick über das BEPS-Projekt von OECD und G20*, https://www.bundesfinanzministerium.de/Content/DE/Standardartikel/Themen/Steuern/2017-06-07-beps-gewinnkuerzung-und-gewinnverlagerung.html (accessed February 2, 2022).
57. Bundesministerium für Finanzen, *Reform der internationalen Unternehmensbesteuerung kommt*, https://www.bundesfinanzministerium.de/Content/DE/Standardartikel/Themen/Steuern/Internationales_Steuerrecht/BEPS/schaedlichen-steuerwettbewerb-bekaempfen.html (accessed January 2, 2022).

would then have to be unanimously approved in the EU Council of Ministers in order to enter into force in 2023.

According to the German Finance Ministry, the background to the G20 countries' action is that the increasing digitization of the economy and the resulting changes in value creation processes undoubtedly represent one of the greatest challenges to international taxation principles. Intangible assets and cross-border services allow companies to operate in states without a physical presence, thus generating profits that they do not need to pay tax on locally under previous taxation principles. Digitization also facilitates aggressive tax planning, for example, by shifting profits from high to low tax jurisdictions. This makes it more difficult to accept the current regulations, and encourages excessive tax-cutting competition in the sense of a "race-to-the-bottom" between states.

The importance of a uniform global solution is shown, among other things, by the parallel deliberations of the European Commission on a digital tax for technology companies. Currently, these plans are on hold, as the approach described by the G20/OECD would probably solve the identified problem areas from the EU Commission's point of view. If no agreement is reached, the program and presumably many others around the world, would gain momentum again.[58]

In addition to the regulations on income tax, transfer prices, and digital permanent establishments, the value added tax is an essential type of tax that must be taken into account, if a company wants to participate in digital platforms. Value added tax (VAT) law is complex and varies by country. Ongoing national and international case law and new or amended international directives, for example, from the EU, ensure that the legal framework is constantly changing.[59] There has still been no international harmonization of VAT rates[60]. In addition, VAT management for mass transactions is administratively very complex. Small mistakes, if not recognized in time, can therefore have serious consequences for companies. Penalty and liability risks can arise from a shortfall as little as EUR 50,001.[61] In order to be able to apply the applicable VAT law, it is necessary to check whether one is in a B2B, B2C, or C2C relationship, whether a transaction is purely national or cross-border within the EU or with a third country, and whether the traded good is in physical, digital (including services), or hybrid form.[62]

Once again, the taxation of digital goods and services in an international context is one of the greatest challenges for the existing legal framework. The regulatory

58. Absatzwirtschaft, *EU-Kommission legt Pläne für Digitalsteuer auf Eis,* https://www.absatzwirtschaft.de/eu-kommission-legt-plaene-fuer-digitalsteuer-auf-eis-180761/ (accessed February 2, 2022).
59. Steuernetz.de, *KPMG-Umfrage: Viele Unternehmen durch komplexes Umsatzsteuerrecht überfordert,* https://www.steuernetz.de/steuern/news/kpmg-umfrage-viele-unternehmen-durch-komplexes-umsatzsteuerrecht-ueberfordert (accessed February 2, 2022).
60. HK Hamburg, *Umsatzsteuersätze in der Europäischen Union und in Drittstaaten,* https://www.hk24.de/produktmarken/beratung-service/recht-und-steuern/steuerrecht/umsatzsteuer-mehrwertsteuer/umsatzsteuer-mehrwertsteuer-international/warenhandel/umsatzsteuersaetze-eu-drittstaaten-1167702 (accessed February 2, 2022).
61. André Boer, *Die Reform der steuerrechtlichen Selbstanzeige,* 23 ReWir (2014).
62. EUR-Lex, *Richtlinie 2006/112/EG des Rates vom 28. November 2006 über das gemeinsame Mehrwertsteuersystem,* https://eur-lex.europa.eu/legal-content/DE/TXT/?uri=CELEX:02006L0112-20190116 (accessed February 2, 2022).

framework is correspondingly complex and therefore, risky. This is particularly true in the B2B sector, and thus, for digital B2B platform models. When participating in digital platforms, companies can be guided by a large number of laws and existing case law. Nevertheless, each participation and each process must be examined and managed, in detail, in order to be able to comprehensively take the requirements into account. In the case of purely digital platform models, this task is much more difficult, as it is more challenging than in the case of physical products to monitor business activities, for example, whether a B2B or B2C customer relationship exists, where consumption actually takes place and where value is added, and the VAT-relevant signs can change rapidly and agilely.

3.4 Tax Audits and International Cooperation Between Tax Administrations

In addition to the legal foundations of economic activities in a digitized ecosystem, monitoring and auditing play a crucial role for companies, politicians, and their tax administrations. It is necessary to ensure planning and legal certainty for companies. Equally, the fair competition must be ensured. For the states, it is a question of the economic success of the location and the safeguarding of the tax revenues to which they are entitled. To reiterate, the international OECD and the EU Commission are in the process of implementing corresponding regulations and mechanisms.

Double taxation should be excluded as far as possible. Tax disputes in an international context are usually protracted and labor-intensive for all parties involved. It is, therefore, important to identify these cases at an early stage, in order to create preventive scope for action or, in the best of all cases, to be able to avoid these scenarios altogether. For this reason, the OECD has launched a "Tax Certainty Agenda."[63] The initiative includes the International Compliance Assurance Programme (ICAP 2.0), the regulations on Advanced Pricing Agreements (APA) and extended joint audit mechanisms.

The European Commission is waiting in parallel with the so-called DAC7 Directive. In March 2021, the Council of the European Union adopted new rules to strengthen administrative cooperation and to include sales via digital platforms. Among other things, the new rules are intended to enable the automated exchange of information between states and their tax administrations, thereby increasing the transparency of tax bases. The rules apply inside and outside the EU and will come into force on January 1, 2023.[64] DAC7, therefore, extends the effect of the tax transparency rules to digital platforms. The providers of digital platforms are to be obliged to provide

63. Cedric von der Hellen, *Die „Tax Certainty Agenda" der OECD – Mehrwert für Unternehmen*, https://bdi.eu/artikel/news/die-tax-certainty-agenda-der-oecd-mehrwert-fuer-unternehmen/ (accessed February 2, 2022).
64. Europäischer Rat, *Besteuerung: Rat nimmt neue Vorschriften zur Stärkung der Verwaltungszusammenarbeit und zur Einbeziehung des Verkaufs über digitale Plattformen an*, https://www.consilium.europa.eu/de/press/press-releases/2021/03/22/taxation-council-adopts-new-rules-to-strengthen-administrative-cooperation-and-include-sales-through-digital-platforms/ (accessed February 2, 2022).

early information to the respective competent authority of their member state about the sellers of their platforms, who are subject to reporting requirements.[65]

DAC7 also explicitly strengthens the audit instrument of joint audits with the aim of being able to process cross-border audit cases involving several tax administrations in a timely, transparent, and legally secure manner.[66]

4 DIGITAL TRANSFORMATION

4.1 Understanding

In this Chapter, we understand digital transformation as the process of changing a company, using the potentials of information and communication technology for innovations of the business model, products, and services as well as processes and organizational structures to make them more competitive. Digital transformation is a process of changing a company or part of a company that requires active leadership and is usually very challenging.

In this Chapter, we structure the process of digital transformation based on the ideas of Lewin[67] into the three phases: "Unfreezing," "Moving" and "Refreezing." "Unfreezing" stands for preparing for the change, "Moving" stands for the actual change process, and "Refreezing" for stabilizing the organization after the change process.

4.2 Unfreezing

The central element of "Unfreezing" is preparing for digital transformation. In concrete terms, this means that managers at all levels of a company and employees recognize that there is no alternative to digitization. Digitization permanently restructures the economy and society. There is no going back to vinyl records, video cassettes, or classic old bookstores. Depending on the industry and region, digitization will occur more quickly, but over time, the entire economy and society will be affected.

The corporate tax department is affected by digitization in two ways. On the one hand, the digitization of a business model, products, and services can have a major impact on the taxation of a company, and on the other hand, it is about the digital transformation of the corporate tax departments. Both directions are interconnected. New completely digital business models place high demands on digitization, especially the automation of the calculation of taxes.

65. Rödl & Partner, *Neue Meldepflicht über Nutzer von digitalen Plattformen: DAC 7 angenommen*, https://www.roedl.de/themen/dac7-neue-meldepflicht-nutzer-digitale-plattformen (accessed February 2, 2022).
66. Steuerboard, *DAC 7: Neuer „Rechtsschub" für Joint Audits*, https://blog.handelsblatt.com/steuerboard/2021/04/08/dac-7-neuer-rechtsschub-fuer-joint-audits/ (accessed February 2, 2022).
67. Kurt Lewin: Frontiers in group dynamics, *Concept, method and reality in social science. Social equilibria and social change*. (Human Relations, Bd. 1, Nr. 1, 1947), ISSN 1573-9716.

Awareness of the need for digital transformation is heightened when companies compare themselves with competitors and also companies from other industries. These analyses can be commissioned from experts, carried out by talking to friendly companies or by attending specialist events. There are numerous studies available from consulting firms, media companies, and academia that show the need for action. Beyond innovation projects, it is important to closely monitor the legal basis and its changes. In the case of regulations, there are constantly new legal provisions or changes to existing regulations that have a mandatory character.

"Unfreezing" is only successful if the rational realization that digital transformation is necessary creates a positive mood for this change process. For many employees, at all hierarchical levels, it is not easy to see the digital transformation in a positive light. They rightly fear that there will not only be winners but also losers in this change process. It has proven successful that external consultants, experts, or coaches accompany this phase.

4.3 Moving

The phase "Moving" is about planning and implementing the intended change process and ensuring that the projects and measures within the change process have the desired effects. This decisive step of digitization has a start date, but in many companies, no end date that can be set when the "Moving" phase begins. In addition, different areas of the company are affected if, for example, the business model, products, and services are to be digitized. In any case, the IT infrastructure is strongly affected and must be changed in an independent transformation project according to the requirements of digitization.

In the view of the authors of this Chapter, clarifying the framework conditions, the goals, as well as the structure of the transformation project is an important first step. When it comes to the structure of the transformation project, it must be decided whether there should be a so-called Chief Digital Officer for the entire company, or how the responsibilities for digitization in the individual areas of the company, such as the corporate tax departments, should be regulated. When it comes to the modernization of the IT infrastructure, it must be clarified what responsibilities and decision-making powers the Chief Information Officer has and what the head of the digitization project has.

Other important tasks in the "Moving" phase are the examination of the current situation and an analysis of the market and the competition. In particular, dealing with the current situation requires sobriety and, in many companies, a great deal of honesty. Not everything that is conceivable and desirable can be implemented with the existing IT infrastructure and the available human and financial resources. The time horizon for a complete digital transformation can be very long. It is advantageous not to over-dimension the projects and to also make use of agile procedures, in order to be able to demonstrate implementation successes as quickly as possible. Regardless, well-developed project controlling is needed to prevent projects from becoming unmanageable or even being aborted.

4.4 Refreezing

"Refreezing" represents the phase of a transformation project in which the planned changes become routine. The task is to stabilize the company after the change; that is, to go into normal operation and realize the planned potentials. There is a paradigm of constant change in digital transformation. Without continuous use of the results in normal operation, it is not possible to realize the potentials. Specifically, this means that only the business model put into operation or the process implemented will bring the expected business benefits. Ideas, strategies, and projects have no influence on the result of a company, only the implemented and operated solution. It is important to closely monitor even successfully implemented digital transformation projects to see whether the planned business benefits actually materialize. Experience from many digital transformations shows that not all innovative and good ideas really contribute to the success of the company in the end.

5 IMPACT ON THE CORPORATE TAX DEPARTMENT

The digitization of the corporate tax department and the taxation of an increasingly digital economy, as illustrated in section 3, using the example of digital platforms, resulting in at least two new fields of action for the corporate tax department that go hand in hand with a need for digital transformation:

(1) **Tax Compliance Management:** internationally active companies must not only comply with the multitude of tax regulations, but are also required to document their decisions and business activities with possible tax effects and to make them available to the tax authorities in a timely and complete manner. In view of the overall increase in compliance and business ethics requirements and the possible interactions between laws and their structural implementation, it is obvious to use technologies and tools in compliance management. At the same time, a change from digital island solutions to a digital end-to-end strategy seems necessary, which corresponds to a connection and integration of tax compliance management into the overall compliance management system of companies and promotes the emergence of a fully digital CMS. In the DACH (Germany, Austria and Switzerland) region alone, there are currently at least more than 200 solutions for different types of tax and areas of application. TAXPUNK's tax technology tool database provides an up-to-date overview.[68]

(2) **Tax experts of the future:** the role of the corporate tax department must and will change sustainably and fundamentally. Many tax managers are already setting the course for transformation. The corporate tax department should be

68. Tax Punk website, https://www.taxpunk.de/ (accessed February 2, 2022).

much more than a staff unit or compliance management department. Substantially, the thrust should be Value Creation & Business Partnering.[69] In addition to legal expertise, new skills will be required for employees in corporate tax departments in the future. For example, an understanding of new and digital business models and processes, fundamental knowledge of related areas of law, such as data protection law, and IT and technology know-how will become fundamental requirements and an integral part of the job description.[70] Managers in corporate tax departments also have to manage a comprehensive and effective change process. This results in the following requirements for the tax manager of the future:[71] (1) change expertise and change management know-how; (2) strong communication skills; and (3) project experience. Numerous education and training needs, in the tax sector, are inevitable. New courses of study such as the LL. M. program "Digitalization & Tax Law" at the WU Executive Academy Vienna, the Center for Digitalization of Tax Law at the LMU in Munich,[72] or integrated Tax Tech Case Studies at the Faculty of Economics, Business Informatics, Business Law University of Siegen, already take these new requirements into account.[73]

6 SUMMARY AND OUTLOOK

As expected, the digitization of the economy and society has a major impact on the taxes of companies and on the corporate tax department. There is no development in information and communication technology that can go unnoticed from the corporate tax department's perspective. The digitization of a business model can be of great importance, for example, when a digital platform is built. Putting all the facets described in this Chapter together, it is easy to see that the operational complexity for corporate tax departments is already very high and will tend to increase further. International and digital business models meet new legal regulations and audit mechanics. At the same time, corporate tax departments can deliver high-quality financial data sets that can be used by business leaders to evaluate and steer new

69. KPMG, *Digitalisierung der Steuerabteilung*, https://home.kpmg/de/de/home/themen/2021/03/digitalisierung-der-steuerabteilung.html (accessed February 2, 2022).
70. Bernhard Liekenbrock, *Digital Mindset – Gedanken zur Transformationskultur und zum Skillset in der Steuerfunktion 4.0*, 1 Rethinking: Tax 71, 76 (2019).
71. Claudia Schmidt, *Die Fünf Merkmale qualifizierter Change-Manager*, https://www.humanresourcesmanager.de/news/die-fuenf-merkmale-qualifizierter-change-manager.html (accessed February 2, 2022).
72. LMU, *Herzlich Willkommen beim Zentrum für Digitalisierung des Steuerrechts der LMU (LMU-DigiTax)*, https://www.lmudigitax.uni-muenchen.de/index.html (accessed February 2, 2022).
73. Extrajournal.net, *Was der neue Digital-Tax-Master der WU bringen soll*, https://extrajournal.net/2021/04/15/was-der-neue-digital-tax-master-der-wu-bringen-soll/ (accessed February 2, 2022); Universität Siegen website, https://www.wiwi.uni-siegen.de/dekanat/ (accessed February 2, 2022); https://www.wiwi.uni-siegen.de/dekanat/.

(digital) business models. The corporate tax department should, therefore, increasingly be seen as a fundamental building block of a business.[74] In interaction with other business units, external tax consultancies, technology providers and tax authorities, a new tax ecosystem is emerging, which requires new forms of internal and external collaboration. The increasing compliance requirements for companies, especially in the tax area, make it necessary to deal intensively with tax consequences before investing in a new business model. The digitization of the corporate tax department is progressing. New applications for the corporate tax department are coming onto the market, new developments in information and communication technology are being used to digitize processes in the corporate tax department and to increase the level of automation. Data analytics, that is, the evaluation of large data sets using statistical methods and artificial intelligence, will become very important. It should always be clear that not only will companies digitize their tax processes, but also the tax authorities will exploit all the potential of digitization. A statement by former American President John F. Kennedy: "A rising tide lifts all boats" can be applied to digitization. Companies and government authorities will use and benefit from the potentials of digitization.

74. KPMG, *Digitalisierung der Steuerabteilung*, https://home.kpmg/de/de/home/themen/2021/03/digitalisierung-der-steuerabteilung.html (accessed February 2, 2022).

CHAPTER 2

How Business Process Technologies Accelerate Digitization

Jan Mendling

Digitization changes various industries drastically, in particular, those that build on informational processes, such as taxation. Business process technologies play a central role in understanding the mechanisms beneath digitization. In this chapter, we will discuss the general idea of the most prominent business process technologies. We will specifically distinguish automational, informational, and transformational effects that these technologies provide. We will illustrate each of these effects with a case from the industry.

1 INTRODUCTION

It is well known that what is called digitization,[1] or computerization[2] brings about drastic changes to the way work in various sectors of the economy is organized. While

1. Brynjolfsson, E., Wang, C., Zhang, X., 2021. *The economics of it and digitization: Eight questions for research.* MIS Quarterly 45, 473-477.
2. Frey, C.B., Osborne, M.A., 2017. *The future of employment: How susceptible are jobs to computerisation?* Technological forecasting and social change 114, 254-280.

these three terms are often used to refer to large-scale economic changes, they often blur the mechanisms that are driving these changes. Key for understanding these mechanisms is an understanding of what different technologies are enablers at the level of *business processes*.[3]

Recent years have seen the industrial uptake of various information technologies that specifically affect business processes. These include enterprise resource planning systems,[4] business process management systems,[5] robotic process automation,[6] blockchain,[7] and process mining.[8] We refer to these technologies as *business process technologies*. *Tax-related business processes* are specifically affected by the uptake of business process technologies for the following reasons: they are informational, thus, making them an excellent target for digitization and automation; much of the tax-related work in corporations and authorities is strongly driven by explicit rules, facilitating the programming of processing rules; and much of this processing is routine work for a large amount of transactions. This offers the potential for already marginal improvements to pay off at the scale of thousands of transactions.

In this chapter, we will discuss the concepts of the most prominent business process technologies. To this end, section 2 introduces the general ideas of business process management. Section 3 highlights key characteristics of business process technologies. Section 4 describes the impact that these technologies unfold at the business process level. Section 5 discusses methodological support for achieving impact. Finally, section 6 presents an outlook on potential future developments.

3. Brynjolfsson, E., Mitchell, T., 2017. *What can machine learning do? workforce implications*. Science 358, 1530-1534; Mendling, J., Decker, G., Hull, R., Reijers, H.A., Weber, I., 2018a. *How do machine learning, robotic process automation, and blockchains affect the human factor in business process management?* Communications of the Association for Information Systems 43, 19.
4. Klaus, H., Rosemann, M., Gable, G.G., 2000. *What is ERP?* Information systems frontiers 2, 141-162.
5. Dumas, M., La Rosa, M., Mendling, J., Reijers, H.A., 2018. *Fundamentals of Business Process Management*, Second Edition. Springer. URL: https://doi.org/10.1007/978-3-662-56509-4, doi:10.1007/978-3-662-56509-4.
6. Syed, R., Suriadi, S., Adams, M., Bandara, W., Leemans, S.J., Ouyang, C., ter Hofstede, A.H., van de Weerd, I., Wynn, M.T., Reijers, H.A., 2020. *Robotic process automation: contemporary themes and challenges*. Computers in Industry 115, 103162.
7. Mendling, J., Weber, I., van der Aalst, W.M.P., vom Brocke, J., Cabanillas, C., Daniel, F., Debois, S., Ciccio, C.D., Dumas, M., Dustdar, S., Gal, A., Garćıa-Bañuelos, L., Governatori, G., Hull, R., Rosa, M.L., Leopold, H., Leymann, F., Recker, J., Reichert, M., Reijers, H.A., Rinderle-Ma, S., Solti, A., Rosemann, M., Schulte, S., Singh, M.P., Slaats, T., Staples, M., Weber, B., Weidlich, M., Weske, M., Xu, X., Zhu, L., 2018b. *Blockchains for business process management - challenges and opportunities*. ACM Trans. Manag. Inf. Syst. 9, 4:1-4:16. URL: https://doi.org/10.1145/3183367, doi:10.1145/3183367.
8. van der Aalst, W., 2012. Process mining. Communications of the ACM 55, 76-83.

2 BUSINESS PROCESS MANAGEMENT

A *business process* is defined by Dumas et al.[9] as "a collection of interrelated events, activities, and decision points that involve a number of actors and objects, which collectively lead to an outcome that is of value to at least one customer." The key idea behind this definition is the fact that work is decomposed in modern organizations: a specific business goal is achieved with the help of a business process, which is decomposed into a sequence of several activities. These activities, also called tasks, are not just separate steps, they are performed by specialized agents, which can be humans or machines. This establishes a division of labor as much as the need to coordinate the separate tasks. The definition of business processes fulfils this need for making coordination rules explicit, and information systems facilitate the execution of the business processes according to these rules.

Figure 2.1 The Business Process Management Lifecycle[10]

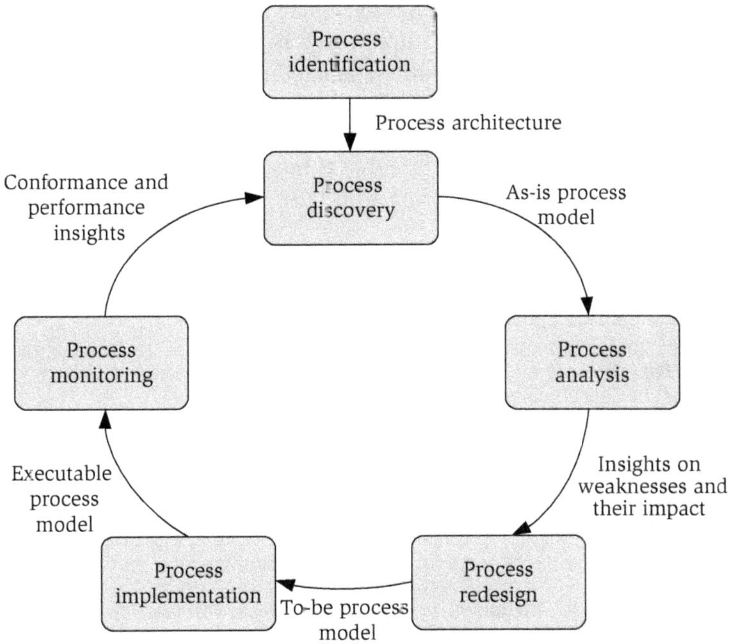

Explicitly specifying the coordination for a business process is not easy. *Business process management* (BPM)[11] is the "body of methods, techniques, and tools to

9. Dumas, M., La Rosa, M., Mendling, J., Reijers, H.A., 2018. *Fundamentals of Business Process Management*, Second Edition. Springer. URL: https://doi.org/10.1007/978-3-662-56509-4, doi:10.1007/978-3-662-56509-4.
10. *Ibid.*
11. *Ibid.*

identify, discover, analyze, redesign, execute, and monitor business processes in order to optimize their performance." Business process models have played an important role in supporting these management activities for more than a century.[12] The different management activities related to business processes[13] are often grouped into six major phases.[14] Figure 2.1 shows their logical connection along with the following explanations:

(1) Process identification: this phase is concerned with the definition of the process architecture and the strategic alignment of an overarching BPM initiative. It can be supported with tools like the BPM Billboard.[15]
(2) Process discovery: this phase focuses on the detailed description of an individual business process. It can be supported by document analysis, observation, process mining, interviews, and workshops.[16]
(3) Process analysis: this phase provides an understanding of the weaknesses and the improvement potential of a single business process. Methods like waste analysis, flow time analysis, and simulation support this phase.[17]
(4) Process redesign: this phase has the aim to define how the business process is supposed to work in the future. There is a rich spectrum of methods that support redesign and innovation,[18] including the redesign patterns[19] and the business process design space.[20]
(5) Process implementation: this phase is concerned with the implementation of the technological infrastructure that is meant to support the execution of the

12. Mendling, J., 2021. *Business process modeling in the 1920s and 1930s as reflected in Fritz Nordsieck's PhD thesis*. Enterprise Modelling and Information Systems Architectures - International Journal of Conceptual Modelling 16.
13. Malinova, M., Mendling, J., 2018. *Identifying do's and don'ts using the integrated business process management framework*. Business Process Management Journal 24, 882-899.
14. Dumas, M., La Rosa, M., Mendling, J., Reijers, H.A., 2018. *Fundamentals of Business Process Management*, Second Edition. Springer. URL: https://doi.org/10.1007/978-3-662-56509-4, doi: 10.1007/978-3-662-56509-4.
15. vom Brocke, J., Mendling, J., Rosemann, M., 2021c. *Planning and scoping business process management with the BPM Billboard*, in: Business Process Management Cases Vol. 2. Springer, pp. 3-16.
16. Dumas, M., La Rosa, M., Mendling, J., Reijers, H.A., 2018. *Fundamentals of Business Process Management*, Second Edition. Springer. URL: https://doi.org/10.1007/978-3-662-56509-4, doi: 10.1007/978-3-662-56509-4.
17. Dumas, M., La Rosa, M., Mendling, J., Reijers, H.A., 2018. *Fundamentals of Business Process Management*, Second Edition. Springer. URL: https://doi.org/10.1007/978-3-662-56509-4, doi: 10.1007/978-3-662-56509-4.
18. Malinova, M., Gross, S., Mendling, J., 2022. *A study into the contingencies of process improvement methods*. Information Systems 104.
19. Reijers, H.A., Mansar, S.L., 2005. *Best practices in business process redesign: an overview and qualitative evaluation of successful redesign heuristics*. Omega 33, 283-306.
20. Gross, S., Stelzl, K., Grisold, T., Mendling, J., Röglinger, M., vom Brocke, J., 2021. *The business process design space for exploring process redesign alternatives*. Business Process Management Journal 27, 25-56.

process. Various types of systems provide generic functionality for implementing business processes.[21]

(6) Process monitoring: this phase focuses on the analytical capabilities for continuously monitoring business processes and their running instances. Process mining technology is increasingly used to support such monitoring.[22]

Steps (2)-(6) are often conceptualized as a repetitive cycle, called the BPM lifecycle. Classically, BPM has been suffering from the extensive effort of documentation and modeling of business processes.[23] Recent business process technologies bear the potential to introduce shortcuts in the BPM lifecycle, once an execution and monitoring environment has been set up. We will discuss these technologies in turn.

3 BUSINESS PROCESS TECHNOLOGIES

Zuboff (1985) was among the first to discuss how information technology affects organizations by distinguishing automation and information.[24] Correspondingly, we identify two general categories of business process technologies: those that *automate* business processes and those that *informate* business process executions.

Technologies for business process automation can be distinguished according to two criteria: (1) how *generic* they are, and (2) at which *granularity* level they support business processes. First, there are systems that offer support for the automation of *domain-specific* business processes in a particular domain. Enterprise resource planning systems[25] belong to this category as much as systems that support customer relationship management, supply chain management, or product lifecycle management.[26] These domain-specific systems support separate activities, as well as their overall coordination along the business process.

Second, there are *domain-agnostic* systems. These are general-purpose technologies that have to be customized to the specific business processes of an organization implementing them. Here, three groups can be distinguished:

21. Dumas, M., van der Aalst, W.M.P., ter Hofstede, A.H.M., 2005. *Process-Aware Information Systems: Bridging People and Software Through Process Technology.* Wiley. doi:10.1002/0471741442.ch1.
22. Grisold, T., Mendling, J., Otto, M., vom Brocke, J., 2021. *Adoption, use and management of process mining in practice.* Business Process Management Journal 27, 369-389.
23. Rosemann, M., 2006. *Potential pitfalls of process modeling: part A.* Bus. Process. Manag. J. 12, 249-254. doi:10.1108/14637150610657567.
24. Zuboff, S., 1985. *Automate/informate: The two faces of intelligent technology.* Organizational dynamics 14, 5-18.
25. Klaus, H., Rosemann, M., Gable, G.G., 2000. *What is ERP?* Information systems frontiers 2, 141-162.
26. Dumas, M., La Rosa, M., Mendling, J., Reijers, H.A., 2018. *Fundamentals of Business Process Management*, Second Edition. Springer. URL: https://doi.org/10.1007/978-3-662-56509-4, doi: 10.1007/978-3-662-56509-4.

(1) At the task level, systems that support *robotic process automation* (RPA)[27] provide the functionality to automate fine-granular tasks that have been previously performed manually by a single user; that is, a human actor conducting work on the computer. RPA systems support the recording and specification of the work steps of these user tasks and the infrastructure to execute RPA programs. These programs are called bots. They interact with other programs through the user interface of a computer system similar to that of users.

(2) At the coordination level, BPM systems[28] offer functionality to automate the coordination between different user tasks. BPM systems typically support the modeling of business processes using the *BPMN* modeling standard and the deployment of these models to an execution engine that executes individual process instances, according to the specified process model. Tasks in BPM systems can be supported by user forms and by service calls to external systems.

(3) At the choreography level, *distributed ledger and blockchain-based systems*[29] support the collaborative execution of business processes of various parties across organizational boundaries. These systems provide a traceable documentation of information exchanges and status updates in a way that no single party can unilaterally and opportunistically manipulate. Individual tasks are not supported by these systems, but solely the overall status updates of the inter-organization business process.

Technologies that emphasize the *informate* dimension are often referred to as process monitoring, process analytics, or process mining systems.[30] These systems take event log data recorded by various, of the above -mentioned, process automation systems as a starting point and provide a diverse spectrum of monitoring and analysis functionality. This functionality helps to understand the process as how it is really executed (process discovery), where it deviates from the specified behavior (conformance checking), which variants exist and how they are distributed (variance analysis),

27. Syed, R., Suriadi, S., Adams, M., Bandara, W., Leemans, S.J., Ouyang, C., ter Hofstede, A.H., van de Weerd, I., Wynn, M.T., Reijers, H.A., 2020. *Robotic process automation: contemporary themes and challenges*. Computers in Industry 115, 103162.
28. Dumas, M., La Rosa, M., Mendling, J., Reijers, H.A., 2018. *Fundamentals of Business Process Management*, Second Edition. Springer. URL: https://doi.org/10.1007/978-3-662-56509-4, doi: 10.1007/978-3-662-56509-4.
29. Mendling, J., Weber, I., van der Aalst, W.M.P., vom Brocke, J., Cabanillas, C., Daniel, F., Debois, S., Ciccio, C.D., Dumas, M., Dustdar, S., Gal, A., Garćıa-Bañuelos, L., Governatori, G., Hull, R., Rosa, M.L., Leopold, H., Leymann, F., Recker, J., Reichert, M., Reijers, H.A., Rinderle-Ma, S., Solti, A., Rosemann, M., Schulte, S., Singh, M.P., Slaats, T., Staples, M., Weber, B., Weidlich, M., Weske, M., Xu, X., Zhu, L., 2018b. *Blockchains for business process management - challenges and opportunities*. ACM Trans. Manag. Inf. Syst. 9, 4:1-4:16. URL: https://doi .org/10.1145/3183367, doi:10.1145/3183367.
30. van der Aalst, W., 2012. Process mining. Communications of the ACM 55, 76-83.

and how process performance indicators relate to execution patterns (performance analysis).[31]

Business processes implemented using these automation and information systems can benefit from a continuous identification of execution issues and their rapid correction.

4 DIMENSIONS OF IMPACT

Upon the foundation of the automate/informate dichotomy,[32] Mooney et al. (1996) define a process-oriented model for assessing the business value of information technology.[33] They distinguish three categories of effects that such technology and business process technology can have, specifically. We illustrate these effects with the help of examples from the BPM cases volumes:[34]

(1) *Automational effects* materialize when business process technologies are used to make a business process model *efficient* by means of substituting labor with technology. The impact of automation is illustrated in a case report by Ludacka et al. (2021)[35] who describe a solution for the German railway operator integrating an Enterprise Resource Planning system, a BPM system, and RPA. Tasks formally consuming 3 minutes of manual work were reduced to 30 seconds of bot execution with error-free and 24/7 availability. With 60,000 task executions per month, the manual work of twenty full-time employees could be saved, yielding a cost reduction of more than one million Euros per year.

(2) *Informational effects* refer to the capability of business process technology to collect, store, process, and disseminate information in a more *effective* way as compared to other means. The impact of information is highlighted in a case study by Buijs et al. (2021)[36] with a Dutch pension insurance. A process mining system was adopted for analyzing the customer journey of insurance customers. The analysts found that average customers call 3.29 times with a

31. Dumas, M., La Rosa, M., Mendling, J., Reijers, H.A., 2018. *Fundamentals of Business Process Management*, Second Edition. Springer. URL: https://doi.org/10.1007/978-3-662-56509-4, doi: 10.1007/978-3-662-56509-4.
32. Zuboff, S., 1985. *Automate/informate: The two faces of intelligent technology*. Organizational dynamics 14, 5-18.
33. Mooney, J.G., Gurbaxani, V., Kraemer, K.L., 1996. *A process oriented framework for assessing the business value of information technology*. ACM SIGMIS Database: the DATABASE for Advances in Information Systems 27, 68-81.
34. vom Brocke, J., Mendling, J., 2018. *Business process management cases. Digital Innovation and Business Transformation in Practice*. Berlin et al.: Springer; vom Brocke, J., Mendling, J., Rosemann, M., 2021b. *Business Process Management Cases* Vol. 2. Springer.
35. Ludacka, F., Duell, J., Waibel, P., 2021. *Digital transformation of global accounting at Deutsche Bahn group: The case of the TIM BPM Suite*, in: Business Process Management Cases Vol. 2. Springer, pp. 57-68.
36. Buijs, J., Bergmans, R., Hasnaoui, R.E , 2021. *Analysis of the customer journey at the pension provider APG using self-service and data hub concepts*, in: Business Process Management Cases Vol. 2. Springer, pp. 111-124.

duration of approximately half an hour, that a larger share of customers call directly after using the web portal, and that almost half of the customers call after receiving a letter. These findings triggered improvements in communication and self-service.

(3) *Transformation effects* emerge from the usage of business process technology to facilitate *novel* process designs and process innovation, with a substantial effect on key performance indicators in comparison to the process design that becomes obsolete. Transformational effects are reported by Pufahl et al. (2021)[37] for the case of a blockchain-based system supporting the financing of the agricultural supply chain in Australia. The system offers financiers trustworthy insights into the harvest assets, reducing their risk, and, in turn, providing farmers with better opportunities of securing liquidity. Up until the end of 2020, asset transactions worth USD 62.5 million and financing of USD 18.5 million have been processed.

5 METHODOLOGICAL SUPPORT FOR ACHIEVING IMPACT

A key challenge for managers is the identification of opportunities where new business process technologies can have a major impact. To this end, various methods have been proposed to support this identification. We distinguish methods that provide procedural support and methods that provide ontological support.

Figure 2.2 The Five-Diamond Method for Explorative Business Process Management[38]

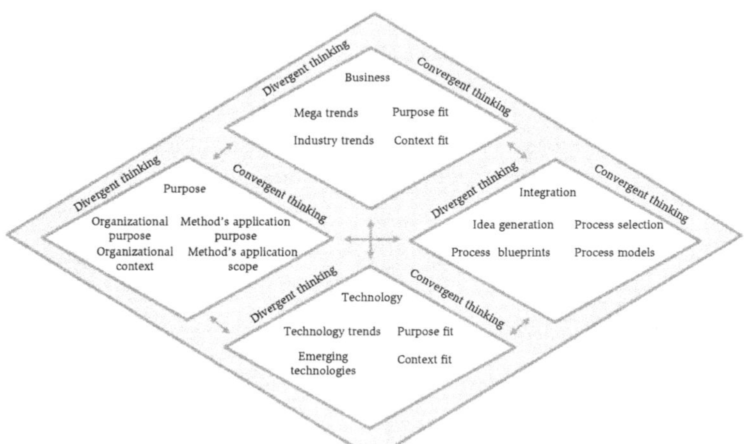

37. Pufahl, L., Ohlsson, B., Weber, I., Harper, G., Weston, E., 2021. *Enabling financing in agricultural supply chains through blockchain*, in: Business Process Management Cases Vol. 2. Springer, pp. 41-56.
38. Grisold, T., Groß, S., Stelzl, K., vom Brocke, J., Mendling, J., Röglinger, M., Rosemann, M., 2022. *The five diamond method for explorative business process management*. Business & Information Systems Engineering, 1-18.

At the level of procedural support, the recently proposed five-diamond method,[39] seen in Figure 2.2, represents an attempt to explicitly consider the capabilities of business process technologies. Each of the four smaller diamonds integrates a phase of divergent thinking followed by convergent thinking. The starting point on the left-hand side is the identification of the organizational purpose and context. The business diamond foregrounds the discussion of megatrends and industry trends. Next to it, the technology diamond focuses on technology trends and emerging technologies. The integration diamond finally integrates ideas and findings from the discussions around the previous diamonds and selects processes for an actual new design.

Table 2.1 The Business Process Design Space[40]

Category	*Design Dimension*
Customer	Customer Segment
	Customer Experience
	Customer Value
	Customer Channel
Product/Service	Scope
	Flow Unit
	Location
	Temporality
Business Process	Coordination
	Trigger
	Outcome
Organization	Objectives
	Internal Participants
	Revenue Model
	Business Partner
Information	Information Source
	Information Use
Technology	Infrastructure
	Automation

The Business Process Design Space is a tool that provides ontological support for identifying new alternative process designs.[41] Table 2.1 shows the six different categories in which the design dimensions are grouped. The idea of the Business Process Design Space is to inspire process stakeholders to think in the direction of

39. *Ibid.*
40. Gross, S., Stelzl, K., Grisold, T., Mendling, J., Röglinger, M., vom Brocke, J., 2021. *The business process design space for exploring process redesign alternatives*. Business Process Management Journal 27, 25-56.
41. *Ibid.*

process designs that they normally would not have imagined in a brainstorming session.

6 OUTLOOK

The above-mentioned cases illustrate the potential that business process technology can unfold, no matter in which industry it is applied. Tax-related business processes can benefit from their digitization using business process technologies for their inputs and outputs being informational, for having explicit processing rules, and having a large amount of transactions. A key challenge is the rightful identification of opportunities that various business process technologies offer in different contexts. Future directions regarding the practical application of BPM see a stronger integration with concepts of digital innovation.[42] The recently proposed five-diamond method[43] as shown in Figure 2.2 is an attempt to explicitly consider the capabilities of business process technologies. Future research is required to analyze the specific conditions and the actual impact of business process technologies in different contexts. The recent five-level framework for research on process mining is a first step in this direction.[44]

42. Mendling, J., Pentland, B.T., Recker, J., 2020. *Building a complementary agenda for business process management and digital innovation.* European Journal of Information Systems 29, 208-219.
43. Grisold, T., Groß, S., Stelzl, K., vom Brocke, J., Mendling, J., Röglinger, M., Rosemann, M., 2022. *The five diamond method for explorative business process management.* Business & Information Systems Engineering, 1-18.
44. vom Brocke, J., Jans, M., Mendling, J., Reijers, H.A., 2021a. *A five-level framework for research on process mining.* Business & Information Systems Engineering 63.

CHAPTER 3

Blockchain in the Tax Law Processes

Matthias Gries

1 BLOCKCHAIN TECHNOLOGY AS A GAME-CHANGER FOR THE MODERNIZATION OF EXISTING TAX AND CUSTOMS SYSTEMS

The exchange of tax and customs information between different taxpayers and the authorities is currently still paper-based in many cases and continues to cause media disruptions. These are associated with high administrative costs and an increased susceptibility to errors due to media disruptions. The current analogue exchange of tax and customs data is also highly susceptible to fraud. Individual measures to combat fraud usually 'only' lead to additional expenses for tax- and customs-compliant companies, while dishonest companies benefit from new loopholes. Digitization efforts, in the field of tax, are currently only thought of in terms of individual companies, although every company is subject to the same legal changes or changes in jurisdiction.

At present, there are considerable technological innovations that should be considered to modernize the existing tax and customs systems. Following the strategy of the federal government, blockchain technology is one of the most discussed innovations of digital transformation of economy and society.[1] With properties such as decentralization, reliability and anti-counterfeiting, it opens up a wide field of innovative applications and new forms of cooperation.[2] Increasingly, the potential for blockchain technology is coming into the focus of tax and customs law. After all, this technology could be used to process a tax and customs data exchange digitally, securely, and in the certified original.

The outstanding advantage of blockchain technology is that it has the key property of unambiguous proof of an unaltered original (even in the digital world). The originality of documents is essential in a tax and customs context, and can be mapped and proven in a forgery-proof manner with the help of a blockchain. The susceptibility to fraud, in the field of tax and customs, could also be effectively countered by the use of blockchain technology. For example, tax crimes such as VAT fraud, which causes annual tax losses of around EUR 151 billion[3] in the EU, or tax evasion committed through cum-ex deals, which has cost the fisc around EUR 150 billion, could be a thing of the past through the use of blockchain technology.[4]

In this respect, blockchain technology requires closer study for the tax and customs area. The focus here is on the use of blockchain technologies, which should be used for taxpayers to simplify tax compliance and for tax administrations to combat tax evasion and simplify verification of tax and customs matters. The first practical national applications of blockchain technology in the tax and customs area, at the level of business, (the so-called taXchain as a research cooperation of the tax department between Siemens and Henkel) as well as at the level of tax authorities (SSI concept of the Bavarian State Tax Office), are welcome.

1. Cf. BMF/BMWi (2021): Blockchain-Strategie der Bundesregierung, 3.
2. Cf. BMF/BMWi (2021): Blockchain-Strategie der Bundesregierung, 3.
3. The arithmetic average of the 2013-2018 is rounded to EUR 150.68 billion. Cf. European Commission (2020), VAT Gap in the EU-28 Member States, p. 9. In 2018, the EU Commission's estimate of the VAT gap amounts to EUR 140 billion; European Commission, 05.09.2019, Doc. No. IP/19/5511, p. 1. In 2017, the EU Commission's estimate of the VAT gap amounts to EUR 137.5 billion; European Commission of 21.09.2018, Doc. No. IP/18/5787, p. 1. In 2016, the EU Commission's estimate of the VAT gap amounts to EUR 147.1 billion; European Commission of 28.09.2017, Doc. No. IP/17/3441, p. 1. In 2015, the EU Commission's estimate as a result of the VAT gap is EUR 152 billion; European Commission of 06.09.2016, Doc. No. IP/16/2936, p. 1. In 2014, the EU Commission's estimate as a result of the VAT gap is EUR 159.5 billion; European Commission of 04.09.2015, Doc. No. IP/15/5592, p. 1. In 2013, the EU Commission's estimate as a result of the VAT gap is EUR 168 billion.
4. Cf. https://correctiv.org/top-stories/2021/10/21/cumex-files-2/ (last accessed: 03.11.2021).

Subsequently, the application possibilities of blockchain technology in the tax and customs area will be presented. Afterwards, the customs system will be singled out and examined for the use of the technology in the customs area, before explicitly referring to the taXchain as the first blockchain solution in the tax and customs area to be applied in practice at the beginning of 2022. In this context, more detailed insights will be provided on the first use case on taXchain in the customs area – the long-term supplier's declaration (LTSD), according to Articles 62 and 63 UCC-IA.

2 USE CASE RADAR FOR THE USE OF BLOCKCHAIN TECHNOLOGY IN THE TAX AND CUSTOMS AREA

The use of blockchain technology is generally only reasonable when several (external) parties want to interact. The implementation of single-company tax and customs processes in the context of a blockchain application is not recommended in terms of technology. In this respect, the following use cases, in the tax and customs area, focus on data exchange between different companies and with the authorities.

In tax law, the focus of the use cases for the application of blockchain technology is on transaction-heavy taxes, in particular, such as VAT, customs, and transfer pricing through the blockchain-immanent tamper-proof and trustworthy transmission of data between unknown actors. The use of blockchain technology is intended to simplify compliance for taxpayers and to combat tax evasion, and simplify verification of tax facts for tax administrations.

In the following presentation, a large number of potential use cases, for the tax and customs sector, have already been identified as examples as in Figure 3.1.

Figure 3.1 Possible Uses of Blockchain Technology in the Tax and Customs Function[5]

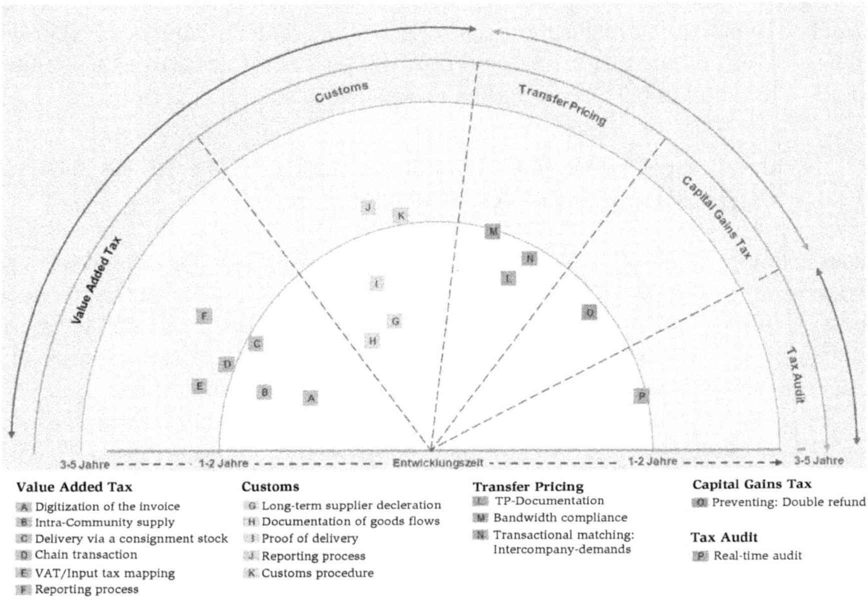

3 ESSENTIAL CONCEPT FEATURES OF A BLOCKCHAIN SOLUTION FOR THE CUSTOMS SECTOR

A so-called Distributed Ledger Technology (DLT), based on a blockchain, is one of the most important technological innovations that should be considered to modernize existing customs systems.[6] As with any new technology applied to existing customs processes, a review of the underlying legal frame of reference is a prerequisite for successful implementation.[7] The following outlines are some of the legal challenges posed by integrating a blockchain process into a customs system. In addition, possible solutions to the challenges are proposed.[8] For this purpose, we first hypothesize the key elements required when introducing a disruptive technology into an existing legal

5. Cf. Risse/Gries, beck.digitax 2020, 394.
6. Cf. S.M. Setyowati, N.D. Utami, A.H. Saragih and A. Hendrawan, *Blockchain Technology Application for Value-Added Tax Systems*, 6(156) Journal of Open Innovation Technology Market and Complexity 1-27 (2020); R. (Robert) Müller, *The Blockchain Technology in Transfer Pricing – Artificial Intelligence and Further Synergies*, 27 Intl. Transfer Pricing J. 5 (2020), Journal Articles & Opinion Pieces IBFD (letzter Zugriff 04.09.2021).
7. In a broader sense, this is illustrated by the experience of the Estonian tax administration, which has been particularly successful in its digital transformation in recent years: D. Jegorov, Technological Advances in Administering Taxes: Will There Be a Tax Office in the Future?, 74 Bull. Intl. Taxn. 10 (2020), Journal Articles & Opinion Pieces IBFD (accessed 4 September 2021).
8. The approach taken is rather general, so that the results can serve as a starting point for a variety of use cases, regardless of context. However, we recognize that country-specific conditions may

process. We then consider real-world customs use case, the long-term supplier declaration, for which blockchain technology is being implemented. Finally, we focus on the various elements of the customs legal system that may need to be adapted.

When analysing the suitability of the legal framework for blockchain integration, three main types of rules can be distinguished. The first two types relate to the existing legal framework, while the third considers the broader impact that blockchain could have on legal rules and even on the perception of the law itself.

The first group are rules that served a purpose in the analogue area, but are now made redundant by the introduction of a blockchain. One example is for any rules that require documents to be notarized (e.g., notarization, etc.). This is an archaic method of ensuring the validity and veracity of paper documents that are no longer needed in a digital environment, where the issuer is part of a blockchain system.

The second type of rules are those that are a barrier prior to blockchain adoption, but either (i) serve a purpose that retains its meaning in a digital context, or (ii) involve an ambiguity that remains even when processes are executed by a blockchain. An example of rules that retain their meaning in a digital context are those that ensure the protection of fundamental rights under EU law; for example, information that should not be shared with a foreign country that handles the data poorly in violation of the rights of the taxpayer and customs. An example of rules that introduce ambiguity would be the definition of 'beneficial owner' and 'sale for export', where the same facts would result in different legal qualifications in different countries or between tax and customs authorities, and courts within the same country. In the case of sale for export to the customs territory of the Union under Article 70 of the CCC, the customs value must reflect the actual economic value of imported goods. All elements of these goods that have an economic value must be taken into account.[9]

Finally, there is a third set of rules that will replace current procedures with the broader adoption of blockchain. This third set refers to new rules required for the implementation of blockchain-based customs systems.

This raises issues related to the technical aspects of blockchain infrastructure and its implementation in law (e.g., the implementation of zero-knowledge proof).[10] This will potentially lead to a shift in awareness from the current legal system, in which substantive rules are applied through legal procedures, to a system in which most of the rules are executed through programs, so-called smart contracts or even so-called smart contracts themselves. In such a system, the law and its technical representation, in computer code, would be almost indistinguishable.

vary-see Wilhelm, Alexander. (2019). Blockchain Technology and the Development of African Economies: Promises, Opportunities, and the Legal Issues at Stake. Law in Africa. 22. 3-42.

9. Cf. ECJ of 12.12.2013 -C-116/12.
10. In cryptography, a zero-knowledge proof, or zero-knowledge protocol is a method by which one party (the prover) can prove to another party (the verifier) that it knows a value x without conveying any information other than the fact that it knows the value x. The method is called zero-knowledge proof. The essence of zero-knowledge evidence is that it is trivial to prove that one possesses knowledge of certain information simply by disclosing it; the challenge is to prove such possession without disclosing the information itself or any additional information, see https://www.expressvpn.com/blog/zero-knowledge-proofs-explained/ (last accessed 9/4/20 21).

The implementation of a blockchain, in the customs system, requires an analysis of the legal framework to outline the legal hindrances, and distinguish between Group 1 rules and Group 2 rules. Group 1 rules require modernization of the legal framework by eliminating redundant provisions and procedures, while Group 2 rules require a debate on how interests will be integrated into the blockchain system. Finally, once these policy decisions are made, the system should be implemented through Group 3 rules.

The processes for deciding on blockchain use cases can be informed by the above analysis. For the design and implementation of blockchain in an area with a large number of Group 2 rules, there is often little political consensus for revising the legal framework. Therefore, legal analysis should be seen as a way to map realistic use cases in advance by looking at areas with clearer rules that involve as little subjectivity as possible. When considering use cases, in the area of tax and customs law, customs and taxes that are applied on a transactional basis (e.g., duties, VAT, withholding taxes, transfer pricing, or excise taxes) seem to be a better starting point than general direct application to profit taxes, such as corporate income tax, which involve complex issues of legal interpretation, and factual information analysis that are often not 'binary' enough to be applied directly to smart contracts.

It also seems likely that any use case of a blockchain in the context of taxation, with a cross-border element, will require some degree of coordination of regulatory frameworks. Blockchain projects are even more likely to succeed if they are implemented at a regional level, such as in the European Union, where harmonization of standards has already occurred or is at least more likely to occur. In addition, some regional regulations are based on premises that mitigate or eliminate the problems posed by Group 2 rules. For example, fundamental rights are less problematic in the EU, because the Union is based on the premise of mutual trust among its Member States that they all adhere to a sufficient minimum standard for the protection of fundamental rights. Moreover, existing ambiguities are more likely to be resolved in such regional regimes, as existing systems of supranational dispute resolution lead to more uniform interpretation.

Apart from regional regulations, such as the Union Customs Code (UCC), the applicable rules or the interpretation of international agreements (e.g., Goods Agreement (GATT), Customs Valuation Code, double taxation agreements) often vary from country to country. In such cases, it is important to ensure that the technology is able to accommodate different material laws and their interpretation. When conflicts arise between jurisdictions (both countries have jurisdiction over payment due to different interpretations, for example), some form of dispute resolution must be possible within the blockchain.[11] An envisioned way to resolve jurisdictional conflicts in advance through the possibility of integrating an advanced bilateral (or even multilateral)

11. Cf. C. Dimitropoulou, S. Govind, L. Turcan, *Applying Modern, Disruptive Technologies to Improve the Effectiveness of Tax Treaty Dispute Resolution: Part 1*, (2018), 46, Intertax, Issue 11, S. 856-872; C. Dimitropoulou, S. Govind, L. Turcan, Applying *Modern, Disruptive Technologies to Improve the Effectiveness of Tax Treaty Dispute Resolution: Part 2*, (2018), 46, Intertax, Issue 12, S. 960-970.

agreement should also be considered. This could require that the reversal of tax and customs results on the blockchain by authorized parties be possible. Moreover, such an approach guarantees some flexibility in terms of the content of smart contracts with a view to adapting them by integrating advanced agreements between countries on the customs treatment of certain transactions. In this sense, the immutability of the blockchain must be addressed: immutability does not mean that the code must not allow an authorized party to undo results.[12] Depending on the use case and the underlying processes, a minimum level of procedural interoperability of national regulations must also be ensured. Overall, the successful integration of a blockchain into legal processes requires the cooperation of all stakeholders, including the relevant authorities, the private sector, and ideally international organizations.

4 EXISTING USES OF BLOCKCHAIN TECHNOLOGY IN INTERNATIONAL TRADE

Traditionally, international trade flows have largely relied on an elaborate paper-based system, requiring physical documents, with original and authorized signatures, to be issued by the relevant parties, and shipped together with the cargo or separately via freight forwarders. Cross-border movement of goods usually involves many parties, including transportation, insurance and logistics service providers, government agencies, and financial institutions.

To illustrate how complex the international trade system can become, one study found that a simple shipment of avocados from Kenya to the Netherlands, in a single container, involved more than 30 different actors, more than 100 people, and more than 200 different documents.[13]

The COVID-19 pandemic has exacerbated the challenges of the current system. According to the International Chamber of Commerce, customers and financial institutions reported some common problems, such as the inability of customers and banks to obtain original and authorized signatures, jurisdictions demanding signed payment obligations, difficulties validating or authenticating original documents, and missing contract deadlines due to lack of available cargo or air space.[14]

The potential digitization of such documents brings about several benefits, from allowing international trade to continue without major disruptions in times of crisis to eliminating non-trade-related barriers, such as reduced costs, increased transparency, efficiency and security, and fewer errors. In addition, the implementation of a paperless system would allow for a smooth transition to the use of a DLT that can be used by jurisdictions.

12. See for a very similar problem with correcting securities settlements recorded in a blockchain: Slaughter and May, Blockchain settlement regulation, innovation, and application, Euroclear, pp. 14-15. The idea is that an authorized public authority could be given the ability to reverse results in the blockchain to correct errors or ensure that regulations are properly followed.
13. Cf. N. Morris, Maersk outlines IBM joint venture (9 May 2018), available at Maersk outlines IBM joint venture - Ledger Insights - enterprise blockchain (last accessed 3 September 2021).
14. For more information, see ICC Digitization Working Group, Digital Rapid Response Measures Taken by Banks under COVID-19 (24 April 2020), (last accessed 1 September 2021).

Current law, in some jurisdictions, currently prevents the digitization of commercial documents and requires physical paper documents.[15] One reason for maintaining a paper-based system is the problem of duplication (i.e., a situation where one party can transfer title to two or more buyers). In the past, paper documents solved this problem because they were responsible for exclusive control. However, with the advancement of technologies, a distributed ledger system has the potential to solve this problem in a more effective way.[16]

Recently, countries that already have regulatory frameworks in place have launched initiatives to apply blockchain technologies to the trade sector. Abu Dhabi Ports, in the United Arab Emirates, launched its own blockchain-based application in 2018 that records and extracts details of transactions, enabling real-time tracking of cargo and documents, reducing costs and time, and increasing security.[17] In 2018, IBM and Maersk started working together to launch a blockchain-based platform that will track the flow of cargo from source to destination, and connect all parties involved in a shipment in real time, significantly reducing costs associated with international shipments.[18] South Korea is currently looking into launching a blockchain platform to integrate cross-border trade and international logistics flows, allowing all logistics documents, such as bills of lading and letters of credit to be stored digitally in a single location and accessible to all parties.[19]

These examples not only demonstrate the potential for DLT/blockchain, but also offer solutions to make international trade safer, faster, and more cost-effective.

5 FIRST PRACTICAL USE OF BLOCKCHAIN TECHNOLOGY IN CUSTOMS: LONG-TERM SUPPLIER DECLARATION VIA TAXCHAIN

5.1 taXchain: The Blockchain Solution for Tax and Customs

The exchange of tax and customs information, between different companies and the authorities, is currently still paper-based in many cases and continuously causing

15. For these reasons, the Law Commission of England and Wales issued a consultation paper on 30 April 2021, seeking public feedback on changing the law regarding digital assets and electronic trade documents. See Digital assets: electronic trade documents, a consultation paper, available at Electronic-trade-documents-CP.pdf.
16. In addition, the introduction of the UNCITRAL Model Law on Electronic Transferable Records (MLETR) could play an important role in this regard, as it would allow e-documents to be transmitted as a single electronic transferable record.
17. Cf. Maqta Gateway, Abu Dhabi Ports launches blockchain technology for trade community (3. Juni 2018), available at https://www.maqta.ae/abu-dhabi-ports-launches-blockchain-technology-for-trade-community/#:~:text=Abu%20Dhabi%20Ports%20launches%20blockchain%20technology%20for%20trade,and%20launch%20its%20ownedblockchain%20technology%20%E2%80%93%20Silsal. (last accessed on 13/07/2021).
18. Cf. S. Jeacocke and N. Kouwenhoven, *TradeLens uses blockchain to help Customs authorities facilitate trade and increase compliance,* WCO News, available at TradeLens uses blockchain to help Customs authorities facilitate trade and increase compliance – WCO (wcoomd.org) (last accessed on 14/07/2021).
19. Cf. T. Il Kang, *Korea pilots blockchain technology as it prepares for the future,* WCO News, available at https://mag.wcoomd.org/magazine/wco-news-88/korea-pilots-blockchain-technology-as-it-prepares-for-the-future/ (last accessed on 17.07.2021).

media disruptions. In order to break up this status quo, the so-called taXchain, a blockchain solution in the tax and customs area, was established and now enables companies certified to raise their cross-company processes to the next level of digitization. The aim of taXchain is to create a better and more efficient exchange of customs and tax data between companies and between companies and authorities. The aim is to switch from analogue to digital data traffic.

In this respect, taXchain is the first blockchain platform that pursues the goal of digitally processing different use cases, in the tax and customs area, securely and in the certified original. Blockchain technology is used here because it has the key property of unambiguous proof of an original. The originality of documents is essential, in the context of tax and customs law, and cannot be manipulated in the digital world by means of taXchain. The taXchain was developed in cooperation between the tax and customs departments of Siemens and Henkel. The term was created from the English words 'tax' and 'chain', which stand for the exchange of tax data based on blockchain technology. The 'X' symbolizes the exchange on a platform; that is, the 'exchange'. taXchain is to be understood as a platform on which all transactions taking place, in the tax and customs area, can be digitally processed by certified companies that want to connect to taXchain (Figure 3.2). The idea behind this is to also share and use solutions that have already been developed by the participating companies, or to develop them jointly under predefined standards. Multiple developments by individual companies on the same topics (e.g., in the event of changes in legislation or case law) and different standards should, thus, be avoided as far as possible.

Figure 3.2 taXchain

taXchain

The Blockchain-Solution for Tax and Customs

taXchain is at the beginning of its development and is intended to digitize a wide range of tax and customs use cases. However, the platform foundation has been laid and the ecosystem for this has been established. The first use case, the long-term supplier declaration (LTSD for short), on the blockchain will be completed and made available in November 2021, after final testing. This is still an active and operational solution for the LTSD, which can be continuously expanded to include the topic of the origin of goods. As the first use case, the LTSD is not only a considerable relief for companies, but also serves as proof of the feasibility of many other use cases and solutions, in the tax and customs area, that are already in the development pipeline.

5.2 First Use Case on the taXchain: Long-Term Supplier Declaration

As the first of various future use cases on the taXchain, a blockchain application for the so-called long-term supplier declaration (LTSD), within the meaning of Articles 62 and 63 UZK-IA, in the customs area, was developed and implemented on the taXchain. According to a nationwide IHK survey, 89 % of the companies surveyed issue their supplier declarations in paper form, which means that this process is associated with high administrative and personnel costs, as well as media disruptions.[20] The first use case on the taXchain solves this problem for the long-term supplier declaration and enables a digital, fast and forgery-proof exchange of LTSDs.

5.2.1 Legal Background

Long-term supplier declarations (LTSDs) represent one-time declarations that are valid for deliveries of goods over an extended period of time, provided that the delivered goods are expected to have the same origin status; that is, simplified, the same production site. In this respect, the LTSD is an important information and evidence document for the direct or indirect claiming of customs benefits. The LTSD certifies relevant master data information for materials between buyers/sellers for up to twenty-four months (comparable to a passport for a material). These are necessary to prove the originating status of a product, in order to benefit from preferential tariff agreements/free trade agreements.

For the possible period of validity of long-term supplier's declarations, which are used in intra-European trade, the following principles, according to Article 62 paragraph 2 UZK-IA, have to be observed:

- the date of execution of the declaration (date of execution);
- the date from which the LTSD is valid (start date);
- the date until which the LTSD is valid (expiration date).

The start date must not be more than twelve months before or six months after the date of issue, but it can be freely selected within this time frame. The expiry date can then be a maximum of twenty-four months after the start date, but can also be freely selected within this time frame. This period of validity makes it clear as to how often these declarations have to be renewed on a revolving basis. The preparation of a single long-term supplier's declaration for both already made and future deliveries is permitted within the framework described above. A supplier's declaration for goods with preferential origin status is a declaration of the preferential origin of goods. The supplier declaration is a document that is normally only applicable in the European Union. It serves as proof when applying for or issuing a preference certificate. It can also be used to apply for a certificate of origin (e.g., EUR 1). Goods that receive a

20. Cf. IHK-Stuttgart, Aufwand für Langzeit-Lieferantenerklärung deutlich gestiegen: Ergebnisse der landesweiten Umfrage der IHK Region Stuttgart zu Lieferantenerklärungen, 2016, p. 10.

preference certificate are, for example, duty-free or preferential under free trade agreements.

5.2.2 Legal Classification of the Exchange via a Blockchain

According to Article 62 (1) sentence 1 UZK-IA, the supplier can provide a single declaration for several consignments (long-term supplier declaration). There is no legal regulation on the type of exchange route or exchange medium. In terms of procedural law, the legislature does not intervene in the inter-company exchange of customs data by means of special regulations. In this respect, the exchange of supplier declarations can be carried out both on paper and electronically. If the exchange is carried out electronically, there are two different options; that is, if the exchange takes place via e-mail, as part of a PDF attachment, there is an electronically unstructured data exchange, whereas, the exchange via the blockchain (taXchain) is an electronically structured data exchange. Article 63 (3) sentence 2 UCC-IA also refers to the electronic execution of supplier declarations and also specifically deals with electronic authentication, which is carried out using the taXchain when exchanging long-term supplier declarations. The electronic exchange of long-term supplier declarations, using the blockchain, is, therefore, not restricted by law. In addition, the blockchain technology even enables the advantage that an electronic exchange via a PDF can be changed afterwards, while the data in the blockchain cannot be changed and is, therefore, forgery-proof (every change, no matter how small, leads to a complete change in the hash value). Even if the data is exchanged electronically using the taXchain, the issued long-term supplier declaration can be printed, in order to be able to provide physical evidence, when checked by the customs authorities.

According to Article 63 (3) UCC-IA, there are three possibilities to what extent the issued long-term supplier declaration can be verified by the supplier:

(1) Handwritten signature (Article 63 (3) p. 1 UCC-IA).
(2) Electronic authentication (Article 63 (3) p. 2 UCC-IA).
(3) Declaration of commitment (Article 63 (3) p. 2 UCC-IA).

With the taXchain, the legal requirements for the supplier are met several times (variants B and C). The taXchain corresponds to an electronic authentication system within the meaning of Article 63 (3) p. 2 UCC-IA. On the taXchain, digital certificates ensure that the acting entrepreneur A cannot pretend to be entrepreneur B and is, thus, clearly identifiable. Every transaction and every block are signed by the appropriate certificates. This ensures that these have also been created or checked by the respective entrepreneurs. The taXchain systemically prevents any possible fraud. In addition, companies that want to use the LTSD use case, on the taXchain, must submit a declaration of commitment that all LTSDs issued electronically on the blockchain (taXchain) apply as if they were handwritten.

5.2.3 Current Versus Future Process

The exchange between companies is still most often in paper form, and less often in file form, as PDF documents via e-mail. The issuing of LTSDs is, therefore, currently associated with high administrative and personnel costs. Due to the media disruptions, the information often has to be transferred manually to the ERP system, which in turn means that it is susceptible to errors. In addition, an effective compliance management system is required, which regularly checks whether preferential agreements can be used in a legally secure manner. In 2019, Siemens and Henkel together processed 11,916 LTSD documents. This illustrates the enormous administrative and manual effort that is required to enter the necessary data into the respective systems. The current manual process looks like is shown in Figure 3.3.

Figure 3.3 Current LTSD-Process

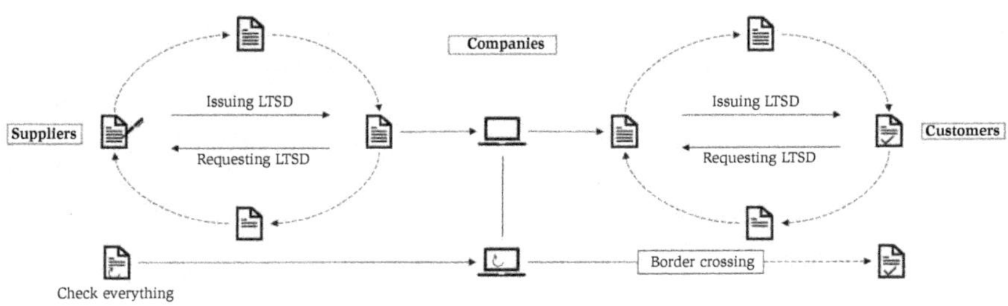

The previously paper-based process between the parties involved is digitized using blockchain technology. Media breaks are thereby eliminated. Query, data exchange, validation and storage of the LTSD have recently taken place via the blockchain solution. The new digital process is presented in Figure 3.4.

Figure 3.4 Future LTSD-Process via taXchain

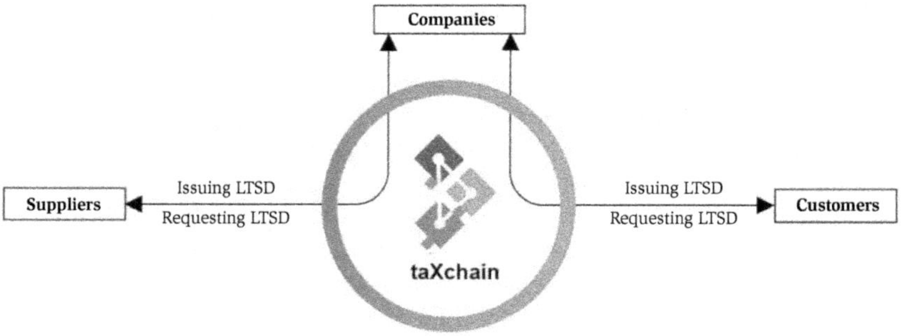

Thanks to the blockchain solution, the information mentioned can be managed quickly and forgery-proof by various participants, as already described. The availability of the data, in the blockchain, significantly reduces the acquisition, processing, and processing times. This enables delay-free cross-border trading. In addition, real-time evaluation of the data is possible at any time. Compared to the manual process (based on the 11,916 LTSD documents), the blockchain-based handling of the LTSD process leads to a total relief of at least 1,600 h/year.

5.2.4 *taXchain Ecosystem, Access Options and Connection*

taXchain is an industry-independent platform. Active participants are also entitled to define new use cases on tax and customs issues and to build on taXchain and to exchange data with companies and authorities via taXchain. Technical developments and implementation can be commissioned by the technology partner or developed in-house.

The development of the first use case 'long-term supplier declaration (LTSD)' as a prelude to the development of a large number of use cases on the taXchain took place together with future users from several companies. This procedure enabled cross-company user-friendliness and system ergonomics, in accordance with the legal requirements. The representations are clear and focused on the essentials with the surface operation being intuitively possible without further training.

In addition to user-friendliness, our overriding goal was to enable a universal platform for the digitization of tax and customs law processes between all companies (regardless of size) and with the authorities. In this respect, the solution is also system-neutral, which means that the use cases on taXchain can be used largely and fully automatically using a modern user interface via web client or, if an ERP system is available, using ERP integration. The connection to the taXchain can either be free of charge by operating your own node or by a node managed by an IT partner for a fee (*see* Figure 3.5).

Figure 3.5 Connection and Access Options – taXchain

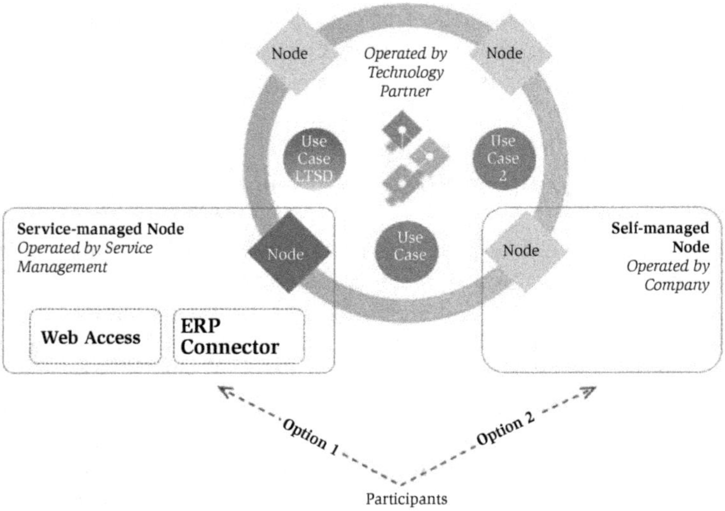

5.2.5 How the LTSD Process Works via taXchain

The functionality can be illustrated using a simple example in the sense of a process cycle; an exchange of an LTSD between Siemens and Henkel is simulated for this purpose. As demonstrated in Figure 3.6, Siemens and Henkel access the taXchain via web access to ensure better visualization (than in an ERP system).

Example: In order for Siemens to be able to manufacture and sell industrial computers, it orders various raw materials, including the industrial glue called Loctite from Henkel. Henkel supplies the glue to Siemens. In order to be able to prove the origin of the goods, Siemens initiates an inquiry to Henkel regarding the issue of an LTSD. Henkel processes the request and issues an LTSD to Siemens. This is required in order to be able to use customs privileges, within the framework of preferential agreements, when selling products.

Figure 3.6 Process Cycle LTSD

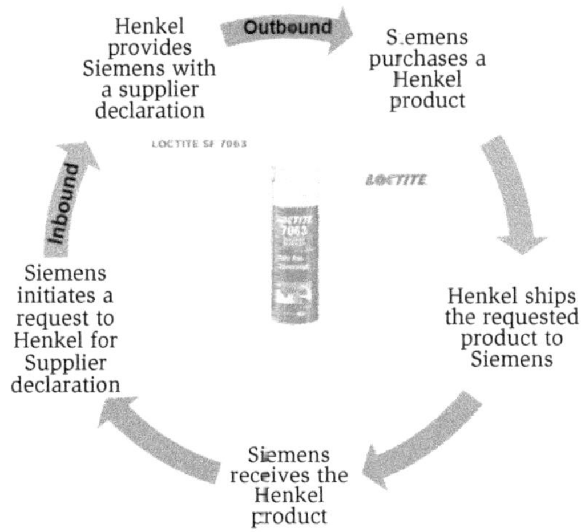

The taXchain can be controlled both via ERP integration and via web access in a user interface. With the latter, a dashboard shows the company the status of the in- and outbound LTSDs and a notification field (with notification, e.g., if an LTSD is about to expire), as well as the user, who is automatically recognized via the corporate ID card. The LTSD process should be viewed from both sides. Companies can be:

(i) a customer and request LTSDs (so-called inbound side), and
(ii) also a supplier and issue LTSDs (so-called outbound side).

The dashboard can be sorted on both sides and according to the various LTSD stages, be a customer and request LTSDs (so-called inbound side) (Figure 3.7).

Figure 3.7 Dashboard User Interface taXchain – LTSD

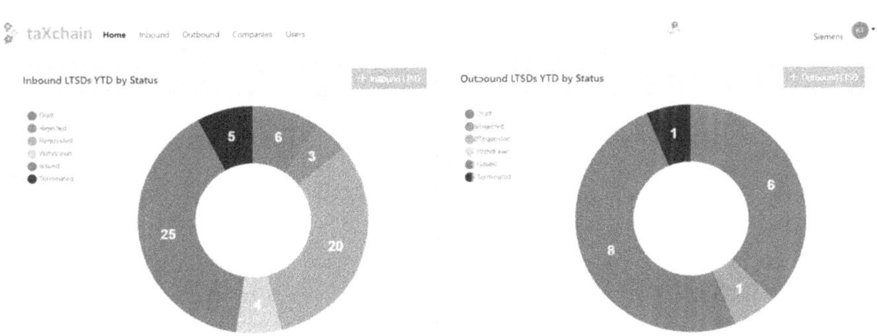

Step 1: Siemens would initiate a request to issue an LTSD using the Loctite adhesive and, in this respect, select the inbound side. Select the data tab with suppliers (whereby the address is automatically adopted) and the validity period, which can only

be done within the legal framework (Figure 3.8). Then enter the customer's material number and trade name in the material tab (Figure 3.9), and send the request to Henkel via the blockchain.

Figure 3.8 Inbound LTSD-Request – Data Tab (1/2)

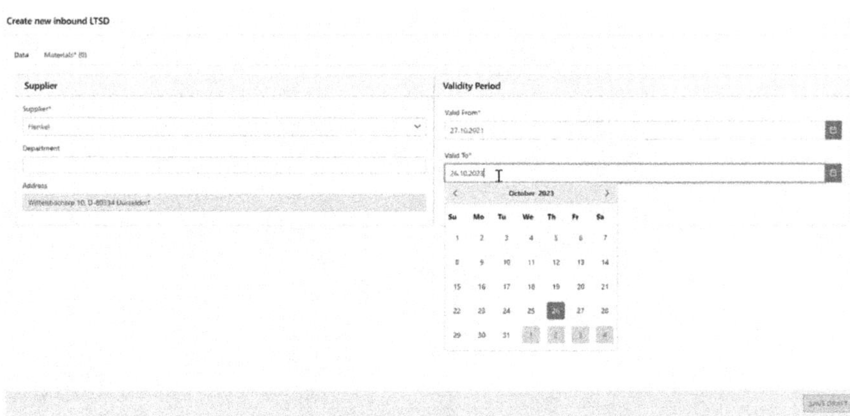

Figure 3.9 Inbound LTSD-Request – Material Tab (2/2)

Step 2: Henkel receives the request via the blockchain and then checks the request and ultimately issues the LTSD to Siemens (Figure 3.10). As a supplier, Henkel acts on the outbound side. In the data tab, the employee is automatically read out via the smart card, then checks the validity period and adds the material number of the supplier, the HS code, the country of origin, region of origin and the preferential countries in the material tab (Figure 3.11). In order to avoid errors, the official regulatory lists are used everywhere, which can be selected as a drop-down menu. This enables Henkel to issue the LTSD, which is sent to Siemens via the blockchain.

Figure 3.10 Outbound LTSD-Issue – Data Tab (1/2)

Figure 3.11 Outbound LTSD-Issue – Material Tab (2/2)

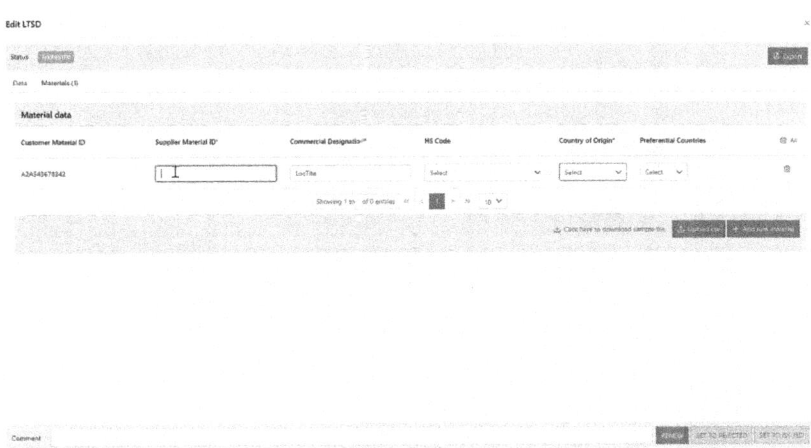

A newly exhibited LTSD from Henkel, using the industrial adhesive Loctite, would then appear in the Siemens user interface. Siemens can also print this out for physical proof at the authorities.

If the origin of the goods, for the material at Henkel, changes due to changes in the production chain, this change can be sent to Siemens via the blockchain. In this respect, Henkel would terminate the original LTSD for one day and issue an LTSD with identical dates, for example, starting one day later. In order to ensure the most time-saving and convenient use possible, there are buttons set up for such cases, which terminate an LTSD in the event of changes in the production chain and automatically fill a new LTSD with the previous data, whereby only the validity period has to be adjusted. There are also various notifications, for example, if the validity period at LTSD is about to end. If the customer continues to purchase the material, the supplier can simply click on Renew and the supplier only has to fill the LTSD with the new validity period (e.g., for the next two years) to issue it. If a company integrates ERP, the replacement of the LTSD can be largely automated over time.

5.2.6 Process Advantages

The customs law free choice, of the use of long-term supplier declarations, is often not used in practice, since the supplier cannot guarantee the origin of the goods over a longer period of time, due to changes in the production chain. Using the taXchain, changes, in the origin of goods, can be continuously recorded and referenced to the respective LTSD, which guarantees the best possible use of preferential agreements in a legally secure manner. Changes in the supply or process chain, which nowadays are sent by telephone, post, or e-mail, separate from the original issue of the LTSD, are a thing of the past. In addition to this improvement, further process improvements can be recorded by switching from the classic process to the digital process via taXchain (*see* Figure 3.12).

Figure 3.12 Advantages of Exchanging LTSD's via the taXchain

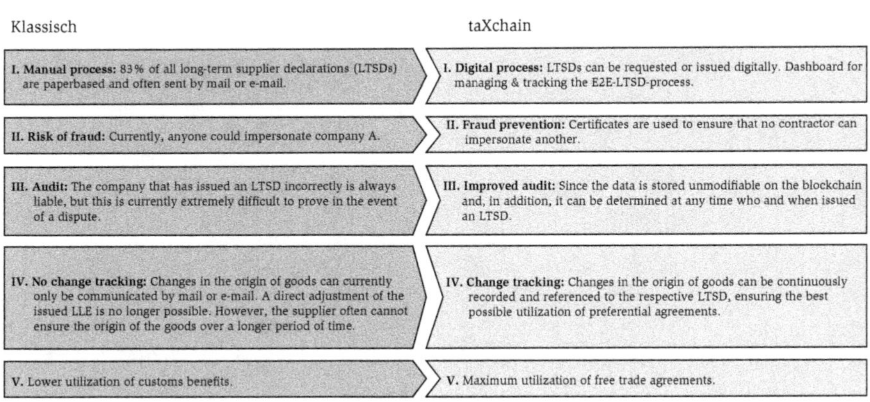

5.2.7 Financial Benefits

By changing from a manual to a digital process, with the greatest possible automation of process steps, time and, thus, costs are saved, thanks to the process design without media discontinuity. The cost of issuing an LTSD is reduced by approximately 70%, instead of the current cost of around EUR 100 per issued LTSD. By using the taXchain, it only costs EUR 30 per issued LTSD.

In addition to cost savings through process digitization, the digital tracking of supplier records via the taXchain leads to maximum utilization of preferential agreements in the company. If a product is sold in a third country, the originating status must be proven by means of the long-term supplier declaration, in order to use preferential agreements. If a correct proof is provided, customs privileges can be exercised. As explained above, however, suppliers nowadays often avoid issuing long-term supplier declarations via paper documents or PDFs, as the origin of the goods cannot be guaranteed for a longer period of time with changing production locations. Using the taXchain, the supplier can digitally make adjustments, at any time, if the origin of the goods changes. In addition to cost savings through process digitization, taXchain increases the willingness of companies to take advantage of preferential agreements, in a legally secure manner, as proof of preference for an LTSD is ensured at all times. Manufacturers can consequently offer the products in a more competitive way or increase their margin by increasing the product price.

Example:

A customer in South Korea opens a new factory and orders 1000 industrial computers from Siemens at EUR 3,000 each = EUR 3 million in goods. The delivery of various raw materials for the production of the industrial computer takes place from different countries and from various suppliers. If Siemens can provide evidence that the goods have a preference certificate, the elimination of the duty rate of 8% results in savings of EUR 240,000, which would have resulted in a definitive charge for the customer.

The last financial advantage to be mentioned is the elimination of archiving costs. Nonetheless, the taXchain has the option of physically holding the LTSD, issued via the blockchain, via PDF print, when it is checked by the customs authorities.

6 CONCLUSION AND OUTLOOK

In order to fulfil the tax and customs law tasks, companies have to fulfil an ever increasing number of compliance tasks, which also cause a high administrative burden. Documentation obligations, in particular, turn out to be resource-intensive for two reasons. On the one hand, the administration works largely on the basis of paper files, and, on the other hand, the procurement of information depends on numerous internal and external interest groups. This administrative effort can be reduced for both companies and authorities through current technological applications, such as the blockchain. The main reason, however, lies not only in the potential time and cost savings, but also in the improvement of data transparency and compliance with legal regulations for all parties involved.

Each new technology first goes through a test phase before it can be used. In the area of tax processes, customs and excise duties, digitization will significantly change these 'fields of work', in the coming years. Moreover, the different types of taxes follow legal mandates or compliance requirements that have to be met. Due to these specified rules, the related tax processes are particularly suitable for digitization. The blockchain technology is not a 'triple bookkeeping' exercise, but a technology that guarantees a completely secure transmission of data In addition, blockchain only requires several people/parties to share this information with each other. This new form of communication results in a significant reduction in the administrative effort required to meet tax and customs obligations.

As a result, blockchain technology can be a solution that meets compliance and documentation requirements, it can be audited by authorities, and streamlines, and automates the standardized flow of information between the parties involved in tax and customs. As a success factor, for the success of the digital transformation, in the tax and customs area, however, we believe that cooperation in the development of technological standards, between companies and authorities, is necessary. Using an interdisciplinary platform for digitization in tax and customs law, traditional replacement solutions from individual companies, which are ultimately associated with international competitive disadvantages, can be avoided and investment risks for technological developments, in the tax and customs area, can be minimized.

Our goal is to establish such a platform for digitization, in the tax and customs area, between companies and authorities. It is important for us to mention that digitization options are system-neutral and company-independent and, thus, developed to the benefit of all involved. taXchain, as a future blockchain platform, for a variety of tax and customs law applications, is at the beginning of its development. However, the platform foundation has been laid and the ecosystem set up for it. This is still an active and operational solution for the LTSD, which can be expanded continuously to include the issue of the origin of goods. As the first application, the LTSD is not only a considerable relief for companies, but it also serves as proof of the feasibility of many other applications and solutions, in the tax and customs area, that are already in the pipeline. The go-live of the taXchain platform should be available to all interested participants at the beginning of 2022. taXchain would like to advance digitization, in the tax and customs area, in the inter-company data exchange and become part of the process.[21]

21. If you would like to benefit from taXchain – please feel free to contact us and become part of it (taXchain.de@siemens.com) or check our website (www.siemens.com/taxchain).

CHAPTER 4

Treating Tax-Relevant Data as a Strategic Asset by the In-House Tax Department

Huibregtse Steef, Jalan Nupur & Verkamman Jasper

---

1 BACKGROUND

1.1 Treating Tax Relevant Data as a Strategic Asset

The power of tax data can be harnessed by interlinking tax technology tools with emerging technologies. Data-driven analysis[1] automation and other tax technology tools provide various techniques to improve the efficiency of tax-relevant data analyses. Considering that data management[2] has become the greatest challenge for taxpayers and tax administrations, in the era of increased transparency and disclosure requirements, combining tax technology tools with the Enterprise Resource Planning (ERP) and other data mining tools would help companies to manage data requirements from different stakeholders effectively.

It has become essential that corporations manage the information provided in various disclosures adequately, as the data provided in many of the reports such as Country by Country reporting (CbCR), Directive of Administrative Cooperation (DAC)-6,[3] Automatic exchange of information (AEOI) reporting is used by tax authorities for various other purposes. For example, the Organisation for Economic Co-operation and Development (OECD) used data provided in CbCR for impact assessment under Pillar 1 and Pillar 2 solutions. Further, for companies that have made CbCR data public, several stakeholders rely on the data of public CbCR for various financial and other aspects as the data provided in CbCR provides a global picture of companies' operations and related financial data. Internally, CbCR can also be turned further into a valuable tool by using this data or combining this data with forecasted/budgeted numbers to analyze various business risks and prepare an early defense for the predicted risks.

Considering the increasing importance of tax data and the requirements of inputs from different functions of the organization in various tax reports, in-house tax departments have to be involved in all aspects of the business these days. This will ease the processes and in timely meeting tax authorities' enhanced compliance and disclosure requirements in multiple countries. Hence, treating tax data as a strategic asset for other functions would also increase the efficiency of different departments; that is, in an ideal system, tax should move higher in the food chain in companies; for example, tax department's requirements of different data points should be kept in mind by the accounting and other teams. Thus, where an organization is introducing finance tech or legal tech, appropriate consideration should be given to the agile needs of data points by tax departments so that tax tech can be combined efficiently with finance tech and legal tech. Figure 4.1 illustrates the significance of data for the in-house tax department, both from a governance and a streamlined and data-driven output perspective.

1. Access to right data for scenario analysis and use of data visualization tools can provide better insights for effective decision-making.
2. Data management includes topics like data preparation, data quality, data governance, data storage, data access and data security.
3. It requires taxpayers to disclose more targeted information about their tax planning strategies.

Figure 4.1 Significance of Data for the In-House Tax Department

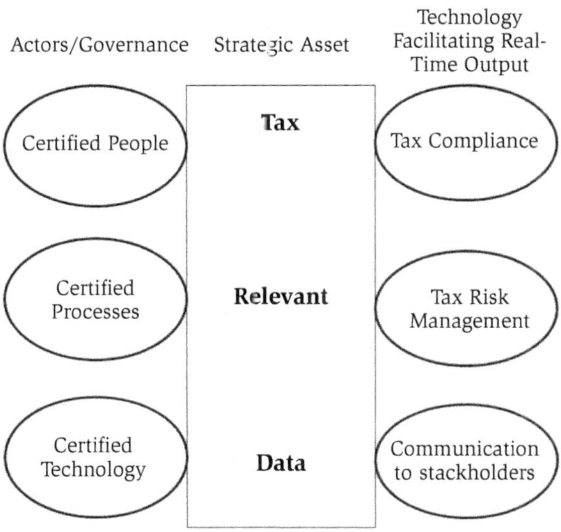

Source: Author's own diagram.

1.2 The Trio of People, Processes and Technology

Internal and external actors of the business ecosystems play an even more critical role in tax. Hence, it is important to effectively manage the needs of all the key customers of the in-house tax department (i.e., tax authorities, management, shareholders, investors, etc.). For this to manage appropriately, the trio of people, processes and technology need to function together: that is, organizations need to motivate people to improve the processes by using the right technological solutions.

Over the past few years, the digitization of tax functions has become one of the primary agendas of in-house tax departments. This can be attributed to several factors, one being the increase in the digitization of tax administration.[4] With increased disclosure requirements and a move toward transparency, tax authorities are transforming existing auditing processes by making the processes digital. There is no doubt that a new digital tax department will rise in coming times: one that will be collaborative, proactive, and data-oriented and has real-time reporting systems in place. To make such a transition smooth and successful, a need arises to inspire and empower people, properly define tax processes and select the right portfolio of tax technology solutions to facilitate this transition. Thus, the "People, Processes and Technology" approach is essential, since many in-house tax transformation projects have failed as the system lacked the required link between people, processes and technology.

4. Example- e-filings, e-assessment etc.

Whenever moving toward digital transformation, MNEs will have to check existing processes in place, assess how technology can be used to streamline workflows and most importantly, encourage a renewed talent mindset and skill set.[5] Thus, digital transformation requires well laid down steps and regular checks to evaluate what works best for the organization, keeping in mind people, process and technology. Hence, this is not just an upgrade of existing systems, it would need real efforts and commitments, as well as the willingness of people to adapt to change and technologies to set the right processes in place. Current skills of tax professionals, including finance, accounting, and law, will no longer be enough, and the tax professional needs to be a fanatic learner. Thus, digital tax practitioner needs to acquire versatility in project management, process mapping, agile methodologies and innovation techniques.[6]

A digital tax department needs to be more diverse and agile. Tax lawyers and accountants will be collaborating with technology experts, data analysts and individuals: a system that will be collaborative, proactive, and data-oriented. It will partner with various functions of the organization to promote its role as a co-pilot to the business (as mentioned earlier in section 1.1).[7]

1.3 Emerging Role of Technology Being Applied to Tax Relevant Data

Already, we see increased reliance and move to adapt to the new technological solutions from both taxpayers and tax authorities' side; for example, a move and support on using predictive, prescriptive, data visualization and business modeling tools. Figure 4.2 represents the different reasons for which technology solutions should be adopted.

5. Aleksander Ogatha & Gustavo Rotta, *Tax, people and technology: Think big, start small*; available at https://www.internationaltaxreview.com/article/b1rhqgp51pfzzs/tax-people-and-technology-think-big-start-small (accessed October 13, 2021).
6. *Ibid.*
7. *Ibid.*

Figure 4.2 Effect of Use of Technology in Taxation[8]

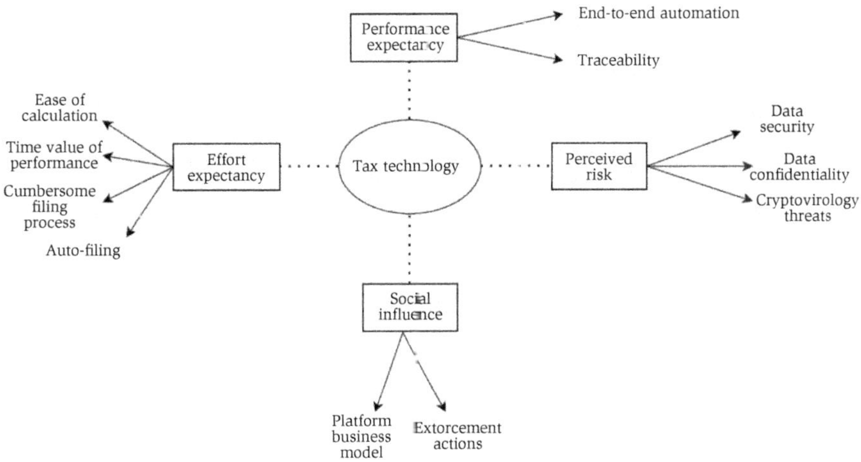

Both tax departments and taxpayers are applying various tools that can help in generating and drawing conclusions and predicting situations from multiple data sources, providing a purpose-built solution for daily challenges tax departments and their business partners face. The control framework can become more powerful to identify, classify, prevent and implement corrections automatically in a timely manner[9] from both an MNE's perspective and tax authorities. A most prominent example is real-time reporting; that is, e-filing, e-accounting, e-matching, e-auditing and e-assessments. Some of the measures adopted by tax administration are discussed in Appendix 1.

8. Primary source: Gangodawilage et al., Use of Technology to Manage Tax Compliance Behavior of Entrepreneurs in the Digital Economy, *International Journal of Scientific and Research Publications,* Volume 11, Issue 3, March 2021 366 ISSN 2250-3153.
9. *Ibid.* 8.

Figure 4.3 Presentation, How Tax Authorities Use Data: The Digital Controversy War on Tax, GTC Virtual Conference, 2020

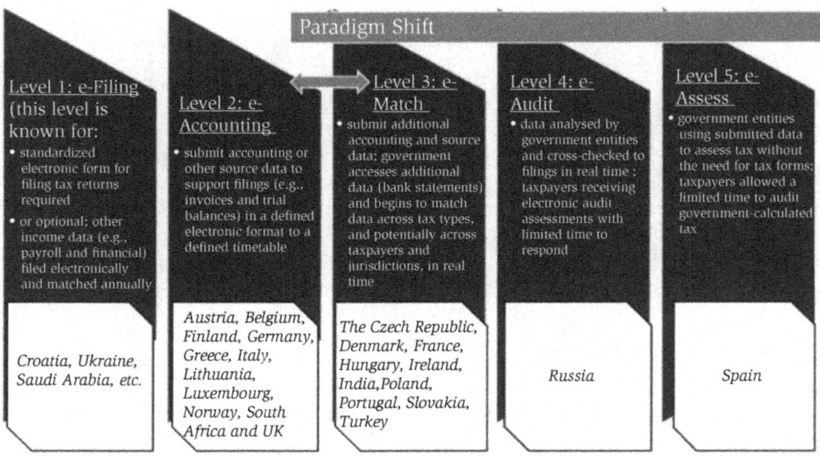

Source: https://www.gtc-global.org/gtc-conference-2020-archive.

With more real-time reporting being implemented in the coming days (Figure 4.3 represents the highlight of country specific initiatives to enhance real-time reporting), we will see tax authorities accessing data directly from the taxpayer ERP and/or consolidation environment, or (more likely) in a data environment that might be extended to third-party sources.[10]

Provision and compliance technology solutions have evolved to automate workflow, data collection, calculations, and tax return preparation and filing. Furthermore, advancements in sharing and storage of tax-related data have improved the ability to respond in a timely manner to tax authorities with accurate information. Various technological solutions can even improve the way tax collaborates with other functions through appropriate data management. Various techniques like Transactional Network Analysis (TNA), the Central European System of Payment information (CESOP) used by the European Commission[11] for data processing and automation are empowering advanced analytics techniques. Further, tax authorities in the different regions are implementing diverse techniques for data mining and automation of the process.

Taxpayers are also exploring new mechanics to deal with increasing documentation and other tax data requirements. For example, Siemens is looking for automation of the transfer pricing process, which shall allow a high-value analysis instead of a

10. Ogatha & Rotta, *supra* n. 5.
11. Camil-Cristian Largeanu, *The data journey: from reporting obligations to advanced analytics!*, in *Applying new technologies and digital solutions in tax compliance (IOTA Book)*; available at https://www.iota-.tax.org/sites/default/files/documents/publications/Books/iota_book_2020_may_applying_new_technologies_and_digital_solutions_in_tax_compliance-online.pdf (accessed October 13, 2021).

mere data collection, including automated end-to-end processes, dashboards with transfer pricing relevant performance indicators in real time and an integration into the company-wide IT—and ERP strategy.[12]

Undoubtedly, all stakeholders have started realizing that technology is a pathway to increase trust, transparency, and risk management. Accordingly, an increasing willingness is seen to invest in skills and advanced tools like network analysis, text mining and web scraping.

1.4 Linking the Tax Function with Other Functions for Effective Enterprise Risk Management[13]

The process of effective risk management provides guidance to the governing board to devise holistic approaches in identifying, monitoring, and controlling various risks that could potentially affect the organization's business.

Companies are looking for more certainty by evaluating how they should benchmark, relative to their peers, to manage their tax operations and risks. This enables them to analyze their tax-risk profile in a better manner for auditors and various stakeholders. The worldwide trend has moved on to improved Tax Risk Management (TRM), enhanced transparency in tax compliances and increased accountability of company decision-makers.

Many MNEs are finding their approaches to managing tax risks unable to keep pace with the overall global developments and increasing legal, regulatory and tax requirements. MNEs have to track country-by-country tax legislation and then cope with such legislation's compliance, followed by handling of reporting and audits that happen subsequently. The debate of fair allocation of taxable profits to various jurisdictions and the new-age unilateral digital taxes adds to the existing complexities.

The best approach to TRM would ensure that the procedures are capable enough for:

- articulating tax lifecycle and evaluating the potential implications of the changes in tax laws,
- evaluating significant tax risks that can arise in this lifecycle,
- laying down risk management strategies, and
- communicating the overall tax-risk profile to top management, business unit leaders and board or risk committee members to assess and oversee those risks.

The integration of TRM with broader risk management framework would help the organization to generate efficiencies and better manage compliance processes, efficiently managing tax processes.

12. Jan Wintehalter, *Exploiting New Technologies to Transform the Approach to Transfer Pricing, beckdigitax -3/2021*, p. 2016.
13. Nupur Jalan & Suchint Majmudar, *Emerging Contours of Tax Risk Management*, in *Tax Prism* (April-June 2021 issue).

1.5 Interlinkage Between Tax, Legal and Communication Technology

Beyond tax technology, as described above, complementary functionalities for digital transformation can be formed in legal and communication/dashboarding technology. The rise in the use of legal technology is transforming the legal industry worldwide, narrowing the gap between law and technology. Needless to mention that the COVID-19 pandemic has been a significant driver of this too, but even before the pandemic, investment in the use of legal technology was increasing globally. However, so far, the use of legal technology solutions in tax areas is relatively limited. Multiple legal technology solutions can be borrowed in the tax area (include tools for document management, drafting that support document drafting for submissions to tax authorities, etc.). Some of the other noticeable examples that came to the authors' attention are included in section 2. These legal and tax technology tools need to be combined with available communication and dashboarding tools and technology so that all stakeholders (internal/ external) collect timely and required information.

In this discussion, a third type of technology is added to the mix of digital resources that strive to streamline data processes within an MNE: tax communication or dashboarding technology. The latter focuses on the communication of outcomes, most likely from systems included in either tax or legal technology, towards respective stakeholders. This results in several communication channels ranging from the internal audit committee to the tax authorities.

Thus, the future of tax entails combinations from various multidisciplinary areas; that is, tax, legal, and communication technology, to achieve the following targets:

(i) as compliance:
  - be on time;
  - be acceptable;
  - be complete;

(ii) as tax risk management:
  - be clear in filing and technical standards;
  - assess nature, quality and materiality of outliers;
  - clear view on the qualitative and quantitative metrics of "uncertain tax positions";

(iii) as communication.

Beyond their communication in a standard format, taxpayers will arrange for communication with multiple stakeholders, for example:

- to the CFO, who would like to know the effective tax rate (ETR), cash tax and cost of the tax functions performed;
- to the audit committee, who might want the same information as the CFO plus the operational impact of tax matters.

The different communication/dashboarding for different stakeholders, to be "real-time" of nature, requires a fully digital dashboard. Figure 4.4 shows a dashboard that combines tax, legal and communication technology.

Figure 4.4 Tax, Legal and Communication Technology

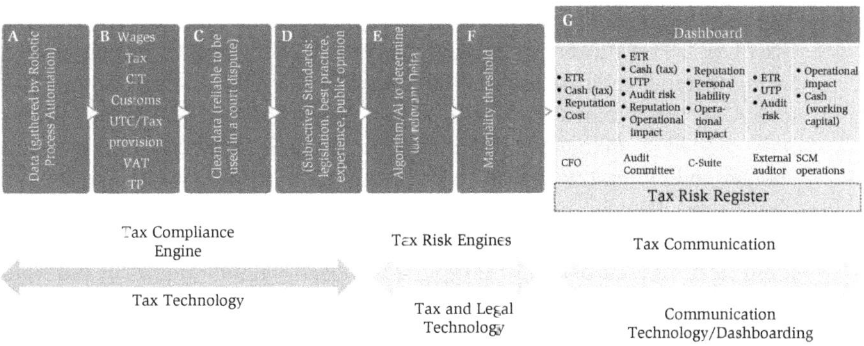

Source: Author's own diagram.

A few observations on the interplay between the three lead processes and the type of technology suitable to streamline and automate such processes are:

- Picking up "dirty data," creating "clean data," conversion to XML-formats to fit the digital mailbox ("the tax compliance cycle") primarily is a quantitative tax technology-facilitated process.
- Making an assessment between "reported tax positions" and "expected tax positions" requires a quantitative tax technology approach at first (e.g., a quantitative value chain analysis). In addition, it requires a legal assessment of facts (e.g., Trail Pad) and how the judge will look at the reported position (e.g., legal facts versus court case decision database); i.e., provide a probability on the outcome of a potential court case.

2 A DEEPER DELUGE INTO THE MECHANISM OF APPLYING TAX, LEGAL AND COMMUNICATION TECHNOLOGY TO TAX DATA

2.1 Tax Technology

In today's tax practice, four generations of tax and technology tools are recognized to facilitate the three major roles of corporate tax professionals: (i) communication with multiple stakeholders (ii) establishing and running a full tax compliance management system and (iii) undertaking tax risk assessment. The four generations of tax and technology tools are summarized below:

- The first generation is performing its tasks on a "standalone" base, mainly covering one or more tax workflows "in isolation."
- The second generation is being integrated into an ERP platform to enhance the data flows and automate certain tax reports and procedures.

- The third generation is taking the applications from the second generation but makes each of the applications separately accessible in a cloud-driven set-up; that is, an i-store for tax applications.
- The fourth generation is driven by a common data configuration for all major tax filings. Tax authorities are only accepting the prepared packages of data fitting through their digital mailbox, fully in line with the predefined coding and XML conversions standards as provided by the OECD. Often, countries have added a taxpayer's identification process, which is more country-specific, allowing any person to log into the tax administration's system and check their already linked information regarding their situation. This link is created by the available data and the identifier of the taxpayer; that is, the Tax Identification Number. An example is the personal income tax in the Netherlands. The taxpayers log into an environment set up by the tax administration and see all their financial data pre-loaded into their tax returns. The data only needs to be validated and possibly additional data that the tax administration cannot be aware of; that is, personal deductible expenses such as health care. Several other countries are also following a similar approach. For example, in Singapore, taxpayers can use a digital identity to interact with the government, including the tax administration and other government agencies.

An advancement in digitization may also benefit tax administrations that suffer from a lack of resources, an issue particularly prevalent in developing countries.[14] Digitization may have a positive impact on voluntary compliance. Real-time or pre-populated tax returns, potentially enabled by well-connected systems and easy-to-access online services, may help reduce the compliance burden on taxpayers dealing with complex and time-consuming tax rules. Moreover, the risk of avoidable mistakes in tax returns could be minimized, thus allowing tax administrations to collect much-needed revenue.[15]

2.1.1 Tax Compliance Cycle

Tax technology tools and software for tax compliance management systems are found in a widespread solutions nowadays. These compliance tools enhance accuracy and ensure timely compliance cost-effectively; that is, they lead to the next generation of compliance features. For example, the relevant laws/guidelines are easily translated into rules for document management and creation tools, which can be used in transfer pricing documentation.

A tool that can be used in the tax compliance cycle is the Document Management System (DMS), which offers increased agility, the possibility of working offline and

14. For an example of a tax administration in a developing country making use of advanced technology, see Aimée Dushime and Akaoma Osele, *Data Analytics: A Paradigm Shift in Nigerian Transfer Pricing*, Tax Notes Int'l, March 8, 2021, p. 1291.
15. David Regan, *Getting to the Heart of Real-Time Tax*, in *Accenture: Voices Public Service blog*, February 23, 2021.

several interfaces to work with. The developments of these tools no longer range up to document security but also include end-to-end document assistance providing services from the production stage and communicating and managing the outcome. This increase in possibilities of the tools is needed as the current documents are no longer flat, static files but instead become sets of (extractable) data that can be structured, analyzed, and visualized by machines instead of persons. It creates a pathway towards more efficiency, yet also more juridical transparency towards the management.

In addition to managing documents within the multinationals (MNEs), the creation of recurring documents can also be automated through various solutions as these match the compliance requirements set out by several institutions and local legislation. As for the first, the solutions in the market are caught in a vast concept of offerings. The range of these solutions is from simple tools that allow tax professionals to create a specific document with a structure, for example, TPGenie. These tools will enable professionals to create transfer pricing Master and Local files in their system through several text blocks and variables, allowing for a quick and easy turnover of the document to the next year of documentation by changing the value of the variable year-specific information regarding the MNE. The other end of the spectrum contains documentation tools connected to other systems, such as the MNE's ERP system, which loads real-time data straight into the document from the source. For example, tax technology tools can extract data from an SAP system through Exchange of Information (EOI) into relevant requirements tax authorities apply in e-invoicing related datasets.

Both are generally seen in other reporting solutions that do not focus on (text) document creation but on financial reports, such as VAT returns and e-invoices. Again, this is a simple example of a quick tool created around setting out rules and regulations, allowing for complete compliance with the tax authorities. As for the document creation tools, the connecting abilities are becoming more and more important as they automate yet another step in the complete process. With the tidy work of inputting financial numbers, human errors are easily made through mistyping or misplacing a comma. Therefore, the fourth generation will ultimately drive the application on an "ERP on Tax" approach. The authors expect that this road map is still a five-year-long journey for the early adopters of technology.

Another example of easy to create tax technology tools is the core VAT or indirect tax solutions aiming to create and file the VAT return in a country based on the available laws/ guidelines. There are various available software tool solutions in the market.

All the available tools have more or less the same purpose, i.e., meeting the compliance requirements in taxation. Thus, the main selling points shifts towards the implementation time, user-friendliness and cost element.

2.1.2 *Tax Data and Tax Risk Engines*

Building solutions in tax risk management requires knowledge of taxation and the necessary capabilities and skills to build such tools/ engines. Subsequently, the difficulty is increased because each MNE uses different ERP systems from which the data can be sourced and used throughout the rest of the cycle. Further, these cycles differ per MNE, disallowing a tool to be implemented quickly and at a lower cost than a solution aiming to automate the tax risk management process. As these tools generally need many customizations, MNEs have to undertake a cost-benefit analysis to make the decision as to whether they want to still use an external tool with the help of the software provider, staying in the Software-as-a-Service (SaaS) model, or move into the development of the tool internally, to create customization, which will only be compatible with their systems yet able to meet the MNE's requirements. A clear distinction between Tax Data and Tax Risk Engines can be made as can be derived from Figure 4.1 in section 1.1. A tax data engine focuses on data for the compliance process; that is, how the data, for example, is gathered from the source, how it needs to be structured to be useful and can proceed throughout the process, resulting in a tax return.

The outcome of the tax data engine needs to represent an economic reality that adheres to guidelines, regulations and rules set out by international institutions and domestic law. Testing the outcomes with these standards indicates that an indication needs to be made that visualizes these standards; that is, through a materiality threshold. Exceeding numbers set out at the start could suggest that the outcome of the tax data engine is corrupted, or the financials derived from the business activities are not in line with the budgetary forecast set out in advance of the activities. This indicates a risk towards the tax authorities as they could start an audit regarding the numbers, leading to a period of (tax) uncertainty. For example, in assessing the tax risk, newer technologies should also filter public datasets, for example, tax relevant data linked to the corporate reputation.

2.2 Legal Technology

Legal technology comes into play when the data shared with the tax authorities do not match the views of one or more tax authorities. A consequence of this result could be the start of an audit or legal proceedings. For the preparation of such juridical processes, such as a court case, there is a great amount of information from existing cases and literature linked to most of the new cases. Analyzing all of these, as a person, will not help in the efficiency of this process; therefore, the implementation of legal technology could speed up the process. Such legal technology tools can be built by using Natural Language Processing (NLP), Machine Learning (ML) or Artificial Intelligence (AI) that allows for a computerized analysis of provided information.

ML includes the use of algorithms, which allow for the processing of large volumes of data, screening these details and gaining insights such as analyzing the data for possible risks. Using ML in the area of taxation is new but aligns with how tax authorities want to organize the tax process.

ML could increase the eligibility for court cases and analytical processes in deriving relevant information, ranging from specific databases to argue a tax case;, to see the (tax) trends of taxpayers in their jurisdiction.[16] Below certain areas where ML can help are mentioned:

- *Data quality*: ML allows for the analysis of large(r) volumes of data, resulting in an increase in the quality of the data and the performance of risk analyses on the set of data based on historical patterns.
- *Tax risk assessments*: ML can increase the efficiency of administrative tasks, reducing the time spent by the tax administration, regarding the collection and building arguments for court cases. This results in more time remaining for employees to work more cases.
- *Fraud identification*: Through picking up patterns from historical data, ML could find an algorithm that suspects or finds fraud from large batches of data. This would increase the number of court cases, yet, decrease time spent on collecting tax money and create a playing field that is the same for everyone, as the chance of bad behavior being caught increases.

Based on a 2019 OECD publication on the "*Tax Administration 2019—Comparative Information on OECD and Other Advanced and Emerging Economies*," forty tax authorities have embraced AI, ten had implemented a degree of AI, seven were implementing it, and twenty-three others were planning to do so.[17]

Examples of legal technology where ML comes into play are as follows:

- *Trail pad*: A contextualized search engine to construe "facts upon which you pay tax"; for example, if there are 66,000 documents, it allows for gathering the relevant facts, court case ready, on the functional profiles of the marketing department.
- *Court case databases*: Allows comparing facts of a case with the same or similar facts in other concluded cases. Most legal documents, including tax court cases, are now available at a few clicks in electronic repositories and legal databases. For example, by entering a list of keywords into a database search engine, all judicial rulings can be retrieved for addressing a particular issue. Some databases also allow clustering of the available information/precedents based on the segregation of topics. Converting long documents into more small digestible summaries is also something that legal practitioners, including tax lawyers, do on a routine basis. By using libraries for this purpose in popular programming languages like R and Python, it would be possible to download the entire content of EUR-Lex (the EU law database) with less than five lines of code. Often, computerized text-mining methods require texts to be in digital form.[18] Web scraping, as the technique is commonly referred to, is

16. S. Huibregtse & J. Verkamman, *AI landscape for tax in Europe today. How Tax Authorities use AI and machine learning to facilitate their tax process*, Journal 84 of the *ICDT*, 2021.
17. OECD, *Tax Administration 2019—Comparative Information on OECD and other Advanced and Emerging Economies* (2019).
18. Arthur Dyevre, *Text-mining for Lawyers: How Machine Learning Techniques Can Advance our Understanding of Legal Discourse*, Erasmus Law Review, 1 (incomplete), (2021).

now the primary go-to technique for collecting data in social scientific disciplines.[19]

- *Web portals and Cloud Systems*: A broad online presence embedded into a governmental portal can be the first step in abolishing the fragmentation of administrative services and promoting the integration of services within a government agency or even across agencies. The information available to one agency would be automatically made available to other agencies, thus eliminating the need for inter-agency requests for information that constituted much of the workload of a given agency in the past. However, due regard must be given to data protection regulations.
- *Word Cloud*:[20] Word cloud is a text mining method that plots words according to their aggregate frequency in the document-term matrix. It is based on compilation of all European Court of Justice rulings up to 2015 (over 12,000 documents).
- *Latent Semantic Analysis (LSA) and Principal Component Analysis (PCA)*:[21] LSA & PCA are closely related to old statistical techniques to arrange large data arrays with better interpretable patterns.
- *Topic modelling*:[22] Topic modelling generates the categories and sorts out the documents after the user has specified how many and what topics the user wants. In topic modelling, topics are modelled as a probability over words and records as a probability over issues. To generate the problems, the algorithm tries to find which probabilities are most likely to have generated the observed documents.
- *Document Clustering with Word Embeddings*: Word embeddings is a text-mining technique inspired by the principles of distributed linguistics: "a word is defined by the company it keeps." For example, Doc2Vec, which is related to the word embedding approach, is a document clustering technique.
- *ODR*: ODR can employ "expert systems" or simple or rules-based artificial intelligence. To create the expert system, the system designers need to acquire expert knowledge from human experts and encode that knowledge into rules which will be applied based on the factual information obtained from the users. This expert system will collect facts from users through interview-style questions and produce answers based on a decision-tree analysis. Also, this ODR system can replace or significantly reduce the role of humans and instead use advanced artificial intelligence (including algorithms, machine learning and big data) to become the third party that performs the mediation or decision-making. Even in Pillar solutions of OECD for the digital economy taxation, this can aid the panel mechanism, though not completely replacing

19. N.J. DeVito, G.C. Richards and P. Inglesby, *How We Learnt to Stop Worrying and Love Web Scraping*, 585 Nature 621-622 (2020).
20. A. Dyevre, *Text-mining for Lawyers: How Machine Learning Techniques Can Advance our Understanding of Legal Discourse*, Erasmus Law Review, 1 (incomplete), (2021).
21. *Ibid.*, 18.
22. *Ibid.*

the need for a third-party panel. Some examples of such systems are used in Civil Resolution Tribunal and online courts in the UK.

- *E-discovery by the use of AI to simplify the process of assessment of documents*: This may include an automated screening of contracts, automated compliance checks of websites, improved contract drafting with AI support, automated assessment of standardized cases.[23]

Figure 4.5 represents the Gartner Hype Cycle that shows different ways in which AI can be used in the legal world:

Figure 4.5 Gartner Hype Cycle

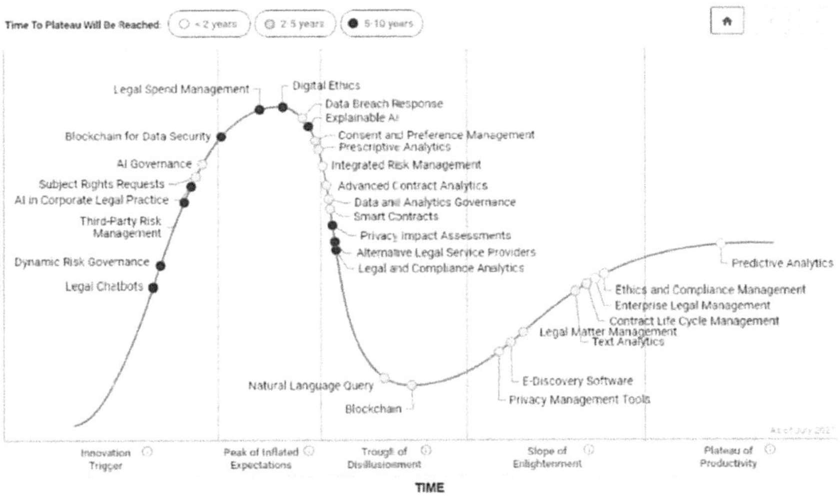

Source: Gartner, July 2021.

2.3 Tax Communication

The need for technology that allows for clearer reporting to stakeholders, in light of potential tax risks, is becoming more interesting. Such technology could be described as "communication technology." It plants itself around legal and tax technology, which has been up and coming in the past years and discussed earlier in the chapter. Communication technology aims to provide valuable information to each specific stakeholder, be it internal or external, through visualization in dashboards. As each stakeholder is interested in different types of information and financial ratios, a division of access to a certain informative flow based on the background or function is key in order to present a clear message to the parties and prevent information pollution. This is the case for internal stakeholders, especially for the communication towards external stakeholders, as the data will be shared through the annual report or website

23. Christoph Sorge, Recent Legal Tech Developments.

of the corporation as a channel. For example, this channel entails a reputational risk that could impact the company, as a whole, and could be tantamount to tax risks in the end.

Tools regarding communication technology have yet to be put in the spotlight individually. However, most technological solutions involving financial ratios or status reports already use visualization through dashboarding. Also, these days with the increase in transparency, appropriate disclosure of tax stories is extremely important. Appropriate tax communication will help in addressing the challenges of lack of communication; for example: a lack of communication and cooperation with tax authorities can unnecessarily provoke a tax authority, even eventually in a possible vendetta against the company.

This dashboard should, in an ideal world, be driven and formally refreshed to allow tax stakeholders to monitor any outliers and/or conflicts on a "real-time" base rather than spending much time in "backing-up" various tax positions taken and in various audits.

2.3.1 External Communication

External communication would mean communication with the key external customers of the in-house tax function; that is, tax authorities, customers, and other actors of the external business ecosystem. Needless to say, some external communication is enhanced because of mandatory disclosure requirements in financial statements or other areas. For example: public companies need to disclose details on the UTPs, their ETR details, etc.

A prime example of communication technology already being used, through multiple channels, is the country-by-country reporting set out by the OECD under Action 13. The report involves three tables regarding information of the multinational group ranging from financial numbers to indication of the activities per local entity. Such a report allows for a quick overview internally based on the ratios set out by the OECD. This information is reviewed internally by the tax team, meaning this would already serve as an internal channel of risk management. Subsequently, upon clearance of the internal team(s), the data is shared, most of the time, with the tax authorities through an XML form, acting as the first external channel that allows sharing this data. Finally, it can be argued that the CbCR data should also be provided to the public to allow shareholders to gain insight into these numbers, as well. An example here would be the British bank Barclays, which already provides a form of this "public CbCR" on their website (Figure 4.6).

Figure 4.6 Barclays Country-by-Country Report

Country Snapshot 2019

		Audited		Unaudited	Audited	Unaudited				Audited	
Country	Commentary	Turnover £m	Profit/ (loss) before tax £m	Total tax paid/ (refunded) £m	Corporation tax paid/ (refunded) £m	Social Security paid £m	VAT paid £m	Bank levy paid £m	Other taxes paid £m	Public subsidies received £m	Average number of employees
United Kingdom	We are one of the largest banks in the UK, with operations spanning all business lines. We have been consistently ranked as one of the top four largest UK taxpayers in the last six years. Various factors mean that the profit we report as being earned in the UK differs from the profits on which we are subject to UK corporation tax. In particular, being a UK-headquartered bank, the profit figure includes dividends received from overseas subsidiaries, which are not taxed in the UK as they have already been taxed in the jurisdiction in which those profits were earned. In 2019, we paid no UK corporation tax. This reflected contributions of £1,231m made to our main UK pension fund and the offset of tax losses brought forward from prior years, as well as overpayments in respect of a number of prior years. In the UK, a contribution to a company pension fund attracts tax relief when the payment is made and, when large contributions are made, this can cause taxable profits to vary significantly from one period to another. The bank levy we paid in 2019 was also reduced as a result of taking into account overpayments made in prior years.	13,717	1,367	1,305	–	412	605	218	70	–	48,241

Source: Barclays, Country-by-Country Report 2019, https://home.barclays/content/dam/home-barclays/documents/investor-relations/reports-and-events/annual-reports/2019/Barclays%20PLC%20Country%20Snapshot%202019.pdf.

Separately, many other companies also have started voluntary disclosure of some reports, such as Shell. Vodafone also went for public disclosure of CbCR reports. Also, on December 01, 2021, a public CbCR directive was published by EU. The directive requires EU-based multinational enterprises (MNEs) and non-EU based MNEs doing business in the EU through a branch or subsidiary with total consolidated revenue of more than EUR 750 million in each of the last two consecutive financial years to disclose publicly the income taxes paid and other tax-related information such as a breakdown of profits, revenues and employees per country[24].

Other than this, companies are cooperating with tax authorities for real-time reporting to tax authorities to increase efficiencies in communication and audit (refer to Figure 4.7).

Figure 4.7 Digitization of Tax Processes

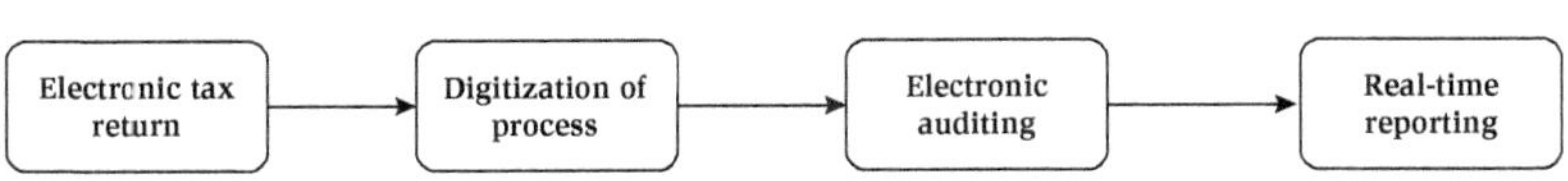

Source: Author's own diagram.

Figure 4.7 represents the digitization of the process and entails the linking of data to tax returns. Electronic auditing deploys inquisitive software on those tax returns, and real-time reporting connects the first three together to audit. For example, in China, the Information Data Request (IDR) was shared with the taxpayer five hours after filing the local transfer pricing documentation with the Chinese SAT.

24. Directive (EU) 2021/2101 of the European Parliament and of the Council of 24 November 2021 amending Directive 2013/34/EU as regards disclosure of income tax information by certain undertakings and branches. https://eur-lex.europa.eu/legal-content/EN/TXT/PDF/?uri = OJ:L:2021:429:FULL&from = EN.

Further, tax authorities across countries are implementing/ experimenting with a new system to have enhanced and better communication internally and with taxpayers. An example of the Hungarian case is[25] that tax authorities signed a cooperation agreement with the Hungarian Language Strategy Institute, and, together with the help of linguists, they seek to analyze the text types and communication situations of the tax authority to identify the challenging area. Further, the NTCA's Clarity Program (*see* Figure 4.8) aims to simplify external communication of tax authorities, by making available communication to taxpayers in simple and transparent form.

Figure 4.8 Communication Strategy Adopted by the Hungarian Government

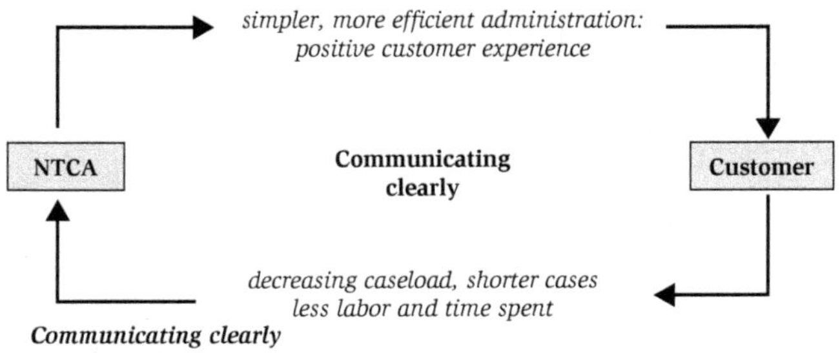

Source: K. Sziklaitax, *The customer has the right to clarity*, Tax Tribune magazine | July 2021; available at https://www.iota-tax.org/sites/default/files/publications/public_files/tax_tribune_vol.41. pdf (accessed October 13, 2021).

2.3.2 Internal Communication

Internal communication would mean efficient communication with different divisions of the organization, which need input from the tax functions for various things, including discussion with C-Suite, investor relation officer, management, and so on.

Several organizations have implemented means to enhance this by automating dashboards with tax data, starting emailers of relevant tax information. Other ways of internal communication as used by some in-house professionals are arranging monthly business tax management meetings, quarterly full tax briefings, and so on. Separately, monthly briefing meetings can be organized with key tax team players, business managers and functional heads (treasury/ account, legal, HR etc.) to discuss the tax matters.

Further, even the CFO would be interested in knowing various tax data points. For example, a CFO would be interested in knowing where ETR is going and, in reality; that is, are they stable, increasing or decreasing. A gradually increasing/decreasing ETR can be acceptable if forecasted, explained to the markets, and is consistent with

25. K. Sziklaitax, *The customer has the right to clarity*, Tax Tribune magazine | July 2021; available at https://www.iota-tax.org/sites/default/files/publications/public_files/tax_tribune_vol.41. pdf (accessed October 13, 2021).

the general understanding of the marketplace and sectors. A falling ETR, when the competitors ETR are rising, may demand careful attention.[26]

Thus, taxpayers/companies are also exploring several ways to enhance internal and external communication with several stakeholders, as they have also realized that in this era of increased transparency, it is better to be more transparent and follow laws properly rather than becoming the limelight in press/ media releases, for not abiding by-laws, or for lack of timely and proper communication.

2.4 New Place in the Process

The place of legal technology, as discussed above, is that this would only come into play upon the delivery of documents and data to the tax authorities, as only then they would be able to make an assessment. However, the future outlook of legal technology is that this would be integrated within the "Tax Risk Management" step displayed in Figure 4.4, section 1.5. As a result, the in-house teams would already start looking at past court cases and other legal documents supporting the reports and results they hand into the tax authorities.

As a consequence of the shift of legal technology into the tax risk management area, the in-house team will need to shift gears and add legal technology to their regular use of technology along with their daily tasks regarding tax positions in general. Additionally, legal technology needs to be either implemented within the tax team, which creates a higher burden of technology on their end, as they are already working with several systems regarding tax technology, or the legal team will have to set up a transition model allowing them to intervene earlier in the process. After that, legal technology can take over most of the current manual work, looking at the same faith of the current profession of the tax employee: technology is taking over greater parts of the process. This results in less room for the regular employee, shifting the description of the current tax and legal professional to the future perspective: MNEs will have fewer employees in their respective teams, with the remaining professionals being either very knowledgeable on high-level specific cases or IT-savvy, allowing them to work with the technology efficiently.

3 REGULATORY AND LIABILITY BOUNDARIES APPLIED TO TAX MATTERS

With all our previous discussion, the message brought forward is that tax is a function in the organization that impacts different divisions in that organization, and to run tax function efficiently, there is a need to move tax up the food chain, as tax function needs data from various functions. For example, Transfer Pricing (TP) in general and TP documentation is not only a tax matter, but several other functional divisions are responsible.[27] Similar examples are found in many other day-to-day operations of tax

26. P. Mason, *Tax commandments for business*, available at https://www.taxcommandments.co.uk/ (accessed October 13, 2021).
27. *Ibid.*

function, where multiple functional teams need to work together to do it right. Some of these filings are listed in Figure 4.9.

Also, as represented in Figure 4.9, the tax department does not always maintain separate risk registers. Even when they maintain the tax risk register, it hardly ever reached the board room. Often, the legal representative and board are unaware of the tax risk area and they hardly want to bring any tax risk area to the notice of various stakeholders. In the past, several situations have shown where the board were completely unaware of risk situations in the tax area, and when the risk culminated, the entire company had to face the consequences. Reputational risk is the major challenge that can occur because of overseeing the tax function. This arises mainly due to unsolicited enquiry and analysis, a provocative and widely published court tax ruling, whistle-blowers, or unfortunate or ill worded public announcements. Often, tax authorities have copious amounts of data. For example, the IRS has published a clear dataset from which tax authorities can easily identify the "most-favored tax planning" location and routes being used.[28]

Figure 4.9 The Traditional Set-Up of Tax Risk Management

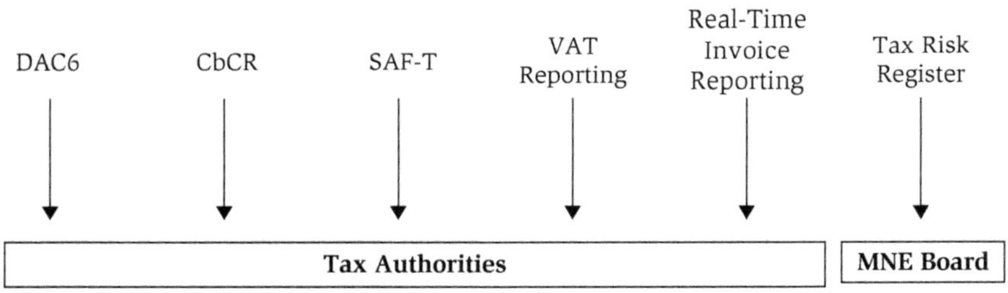

Source: Author's own diagram.

By maintaining an appropriate tax risk register, the broader analysis of various areas of risk can be identified and communicated to various stakeholders. The sort of communication may also provide early warnings, of material tax changes, that need to be undertaken in the UTPs to a different team such as the financial reporting team. For example, question what the board needs to know about Digital Services Taxes (DSTs), and why do they matter now.[29] The broader impact of DST needs to be communicated to different stakeholders.

Further, since tax directly impacts Earnings per share (EPS) and share price, a 1%-point reduction in ETR increases EPS by 1%. Often, investors are interested in knowing any material changes in the tax outgo. C-Suites/investors relation officers should know what is happening in the organization, so tax risks do not come at stake at a later stage. Investors' relation officers would be interested in knowing the impact of tax changes on the P/E ratio.

28. *Source*: IRS Releases Country-by-Country Filings: Insights on Tax Havens, Effective Tax Rate by Dr. Glenn DeSouza, 2021.
29. W. Morris & P. Brown, *Digital service taxes: Are they here to stay?*; available at https://www.pwc.com/us/en/services/tax/library/digital-service-taxes.html.

Further, business people should be aware of taxes in the commercial dealings, helping them close the deal, considering the tax aspects and availing the benefits of the government support and optimizing cash results where possible.[30] The pressing point is whether the limited definition of stakeholders in "talking about tax" is capitalized when discussing tax to the public or discussing tax to the press (Figure 4.10)?

Figure 4.10 Tax: A Game of Multidisciplinary Stakeholders

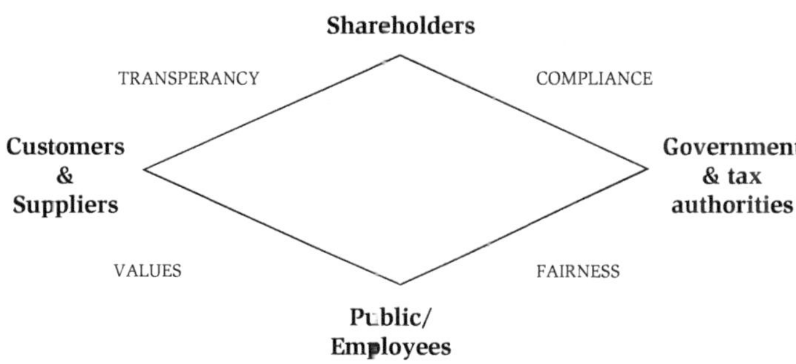

Source: P. Mason, *Tax commandments for business*, available at https://www.taxcommandments.co.uk/ (accessed October 13, 2021).

As over time, tax has become more of a regulatory obligation and the liabilities imposed on taxpayers and legal representatives, it is essential that all stakeholders are well informed, in advance, and any tax issues do not come as a surprise to them at a later stage (e.g., details on uncertain tax positions). This means that more and more liabilities will land with severe financial consequences. For example, a missing or wrong DAC-6 filing, in the Netherlands, is seen as a criminal offence for which the fine imposed exceeds EUR 800,000 as per event.

More so, with the GRI 2007 index or coming into the place of public disclosure of tax data (one such example being CbCR reporting), those responsible in an organization should take care to address and inform the board of any such risk areas. Thus, tax liabilities have to be understood by the board and legal representatives and brought to notice in board discussions through dynamic disclosure policies. As these may impact the public domain sentiments, it also needs to be communicated well in the audit committee. Thus, gone are the days where tax department professionals were not able to make it to the boardroom. With increased transparency, it is time to find adequate spaces for the tax function so that they can bring material issues to boardroom discussions.

30. Mason, *supra* n. 26.

4 TRENDS AND WAY FORWARD: HOW TO INTEGRATE COMMUNICATION, LEGAL AND TAX TECHNOLOGY AS ONE ROAD MAP

This chapter has shown the need for combining tax technology with legal technology and communication technology to meet the needs of different stakeholders, to run tax functions efficiently and take well-informed decisions. In addition, tax needs to move up the finance value chain so that any sort of data requirements for tax purposes are easily available. Further, to implement this successfully and to collaborate with other business teams (as tax departments need to coordinate/ interview different business people for various tax risks) the need for different skill sets in people working in the tax department will be apparent.

Figure 4.11 illustrates the total revision of job titles following the continuous digital transformation of processes facilitated by a host of technologies.

Figure 4.11 Tax Jobs of the Future

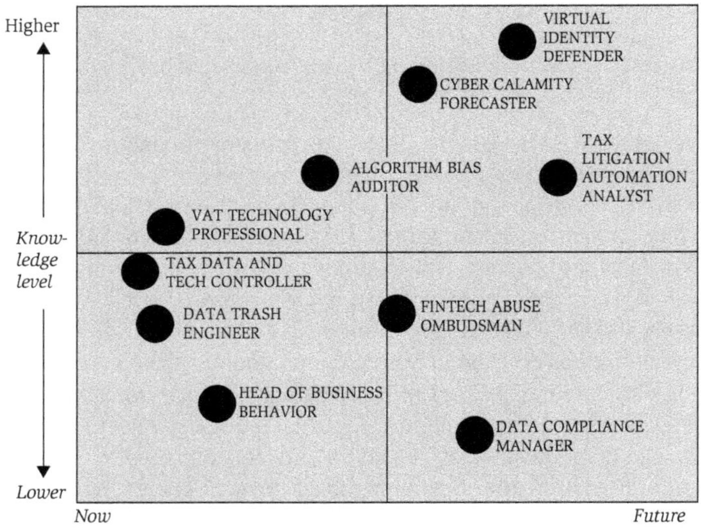

Source: Whitepaper on "The Future of Tax in 2025: A Data Driven Version of the Tax World", TPA Global, 2021.

A very structured manner to define the in-house tax workflows could be using SOX (more regulatory) or RACI (more functional) governance tools to connect people to processes (refer Figure 4.12). The use of SOX control does not per se identify tax leakages and/or non-compliant tax processes.

Table 4.1 Example of a RACI Used in the Transfer Pricing Department

	Head of Tax	Head of TP	Central Tax/Finance Team	Local Tax/Finance Team	Legal Team	Business Team	-
1. Development/maintenance of TP Documentation							
2. Consultancy – Advisory and Implementation							
3. Audit Support							
4. Risk Management							
5. Systems (Central Data Management & Retrieval)							
6. Capacity Planning Insource/Outsource							
7. Global Benchmarking Platform (Outsourced to Third Parties)							
8. Sign-Off TP Documents							
9. Legal Agreements – Set Up and Implementation							

Source: Author's own.

This shift in future jobs towards a generation that can cooperate with IT systems should also be acknowledged by universities in their curriculum. For example, a master education can include courses regarding tax technology, where the student becomes acquainted with this area at an entry-level level, as the tax and legal technology is relatively uncommon to come across outside of the profession. This educational side is also discussed by Barczentewicz,[31] which discusses several perspectives on how this side could be taught to students or current professionals looking to develop this side of their skill set. Barczentewicz mainly focuses on the legal side of the usage of technology; however, these perspectives could well be implemented to the tax technology world as well. The most beneficial technique that could be used in the training and education of tax professionals would be not regarding coding, as tax professionals generally do not work with IT systems at the back-end. Therefore, a soft skill educational approach would be most beneficial as this would have tax professionals understand how to communicate from an overview point of view, align and cooperate with different teams.[32]

The new generation of technology and data-driven innovations are sparking a reinvention of the very fundamentals of MNEs and revenue agencies, recasting compliance strategy, organizational structures, service delivery and relationships with stakeholders.

A trend not yet observed is the use of legal technology to (i) collect the "facts on which base you get taxed," (ii) assess your tax risk compared to other "factual same or

31. Mikolaj Barczentewicz, *Teaching Technology to (Future) Lawyers (November 5, 2021)*. 14(1) Erasmus Law Review (2021), Available at SSRN: https://ssrn.com/abstract=3957137.
32. M. Barczentewicz, *Teaching Technology to (Future) Lawyers*, 1 Erasmus Law Review (incomplete), (2021).

similar" cases, e.g., court cases, Advance Pricing Agreements (APAs), DAC-6 databases and (iii) streamline and communicate your tax risk assessment for quarterly/yearly accounting reporting to shareholders and other stakeholders.

Combining tax technology with legal and communication technology will, thus, help to meet the requirements of key customers of in-house tax departments; that is, shareholders and C-Suite, tax authorities, employees and advisors, external customers, other corporate departments and businesses. Needless to say, strong and effective communication of a tax policy is crucial for tax governance. Separately, there would be an increased efficiencies in current workflows, be it digitization of tax returns, group tax accounting reporting, document management, TP testing and control. Some organizations prepare monthly reports for CFO: dashboarding may do away with the need for such reports.

However, as multiple off-the-shelf software already exists on the market, it is important for the in-house team to comprehensively understand the capabilities of these tools, for effective use of data visualization tools, data management systems and robotic process automation. In-house teams initially can work with specialists to bring insight into the right methodology, creating a vision of the tax landscape, understanding the technology solution available that will be beneficial, implementing and fitting well with the existing solutions.

APPENDIX 1: ADOPTION OF THE TECHNOLOGICAL SOLUTION BY TAX AUTHORITIES

Across the world, tax administrations are in different stages of digitization, with some offering simple online services, such as e-filing, and others performing full tax audits online. Figure 4.12 shows a glimpse of different service offerings pursuant to the digitization of tax administration across various regions.

Figure 4.12 Adoption of Technological Solutions by Tax Authorities

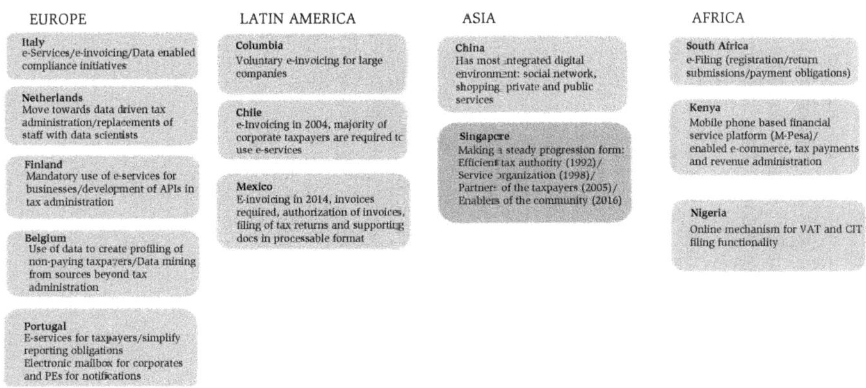

Source: Author's own diagram.

Apart from these, tax authorities are adopting new technologies and deploying advanced solutions for data management, predictive modelling, data visualization, some of which are discussed below.

a. Data management techniques

Some of the mechanics of data management techniques, as used by the Netherlands Tax and Customs Administration (NTCA), are mentioned below.[33]

33. IOTA Good Practice Guide, *Applying Data and analytics in tax administrations*, available at https://www.iota-tax.org/sites/default/files/pub/gpg_project/iota-practice-guide.pdf (accessed October 13, 2021). The figures below from 4.13 to 4.23 are taken from this guide.

Data quadrant model	Under this model, tax administration optimizes the way in which ad hoc models and data are created by their data scientists and look for structured production process. The basic assumption taken in this model is data deployment starts with raw materials and ends up in some form of the product. It further implements the notion of the "push-pull point," i.e., push systems and pull systems.

Figure 4.13 The Data Quadrant

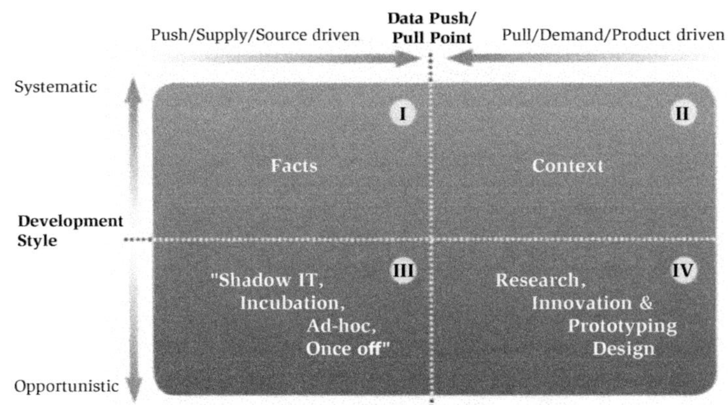

Data layer architecture	Under this, data is prepared in layers. The new layer is built on the previous layer and with different color for functional purposes (as shown in Figure 4.14). This data preparation method helps the organization to focus on creating value adding insights, to have a strong focus on data quality and business validation, a clear data lineage and a common language and shared approach.

Figure 4.14 Data Layer Architecture

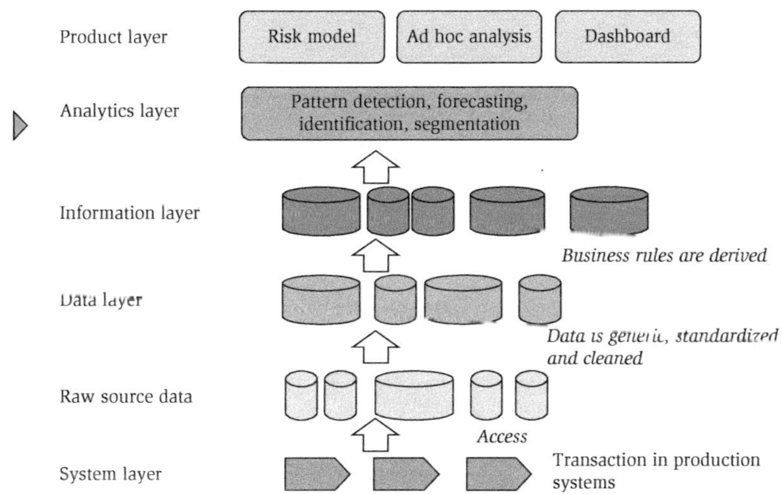

DAMA framework	This is a widely accepted framework for data management that standardizes terminology, processes, roles and deliverables. It includes several topics, like data development, data architecture, data quality, metadata management etc.

Figure 4.15 The DAMA Framework

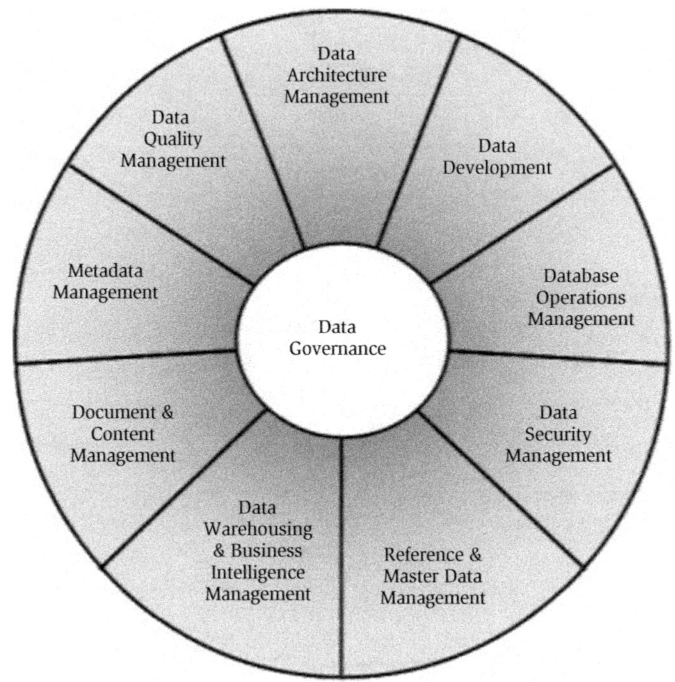

b. Predictive modelling:

Some of the mechanics of predictive modelling are discussed below:

Combine and optimize—Predicting income using Big Data and regression.

The Irish revenue authorities use a model based on regression to estimate the income basis on big data and third-party information.

Figure 4.16 The Model Used by the Irish Revenue Authorities

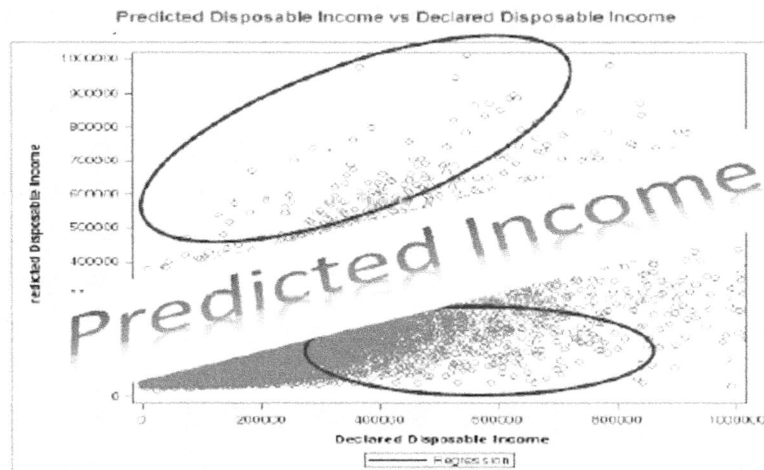

Note: The figure is available online at https://www.iota-tax.org/sites/default/files/pub/gpg_project/iota-practice-guide.pdf.

Combine and optimize—Risk matrix	Tax authorities can use data visualization tools to present information in tables/ charts; these can help in making well and better-informed decisions.

Figure 4.17 The Risk Matrix

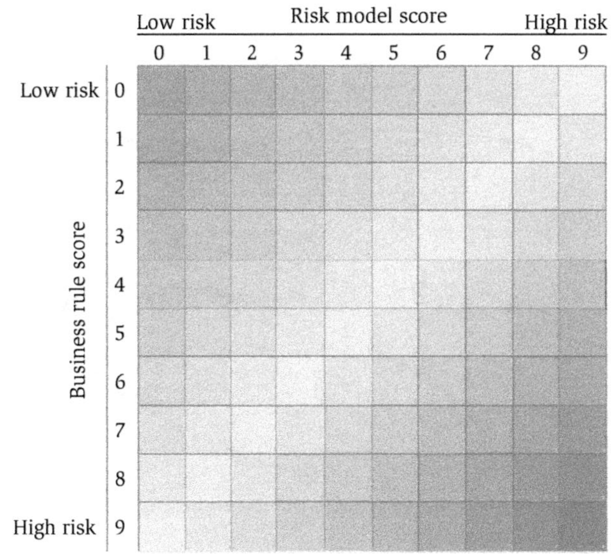

Combine and optimize—VAT risk model	The Netherlands has implemented an iterative approach to create the model. It focuses on VAT declaration with a refund. Risk indicators are the input; a training sample is extracted, the model is optimized on the sample and compared with another one, so iteratively, the model is improved.

Figure 4.18 VAT Risk Model

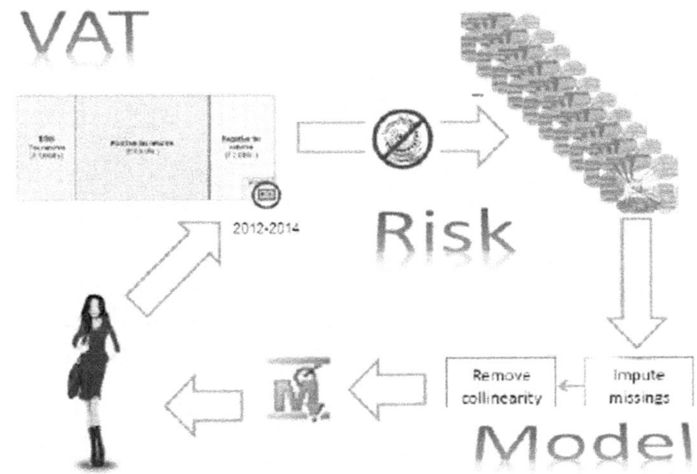

Note: The figure is available online at https://www.iota-tax.org/sites/default/files/pub/gpg_project/iota-practice-guide.pdf.

Risk indicators—Network analysis with Panorama	Network analysis is a very useful tool to detect fraudulent organizations. The tool named Panorama is used by the Hungarian Tax Administration to create networks that help to detect VAT fraud. *Figure 4.19 Network Analysis with Panorama*

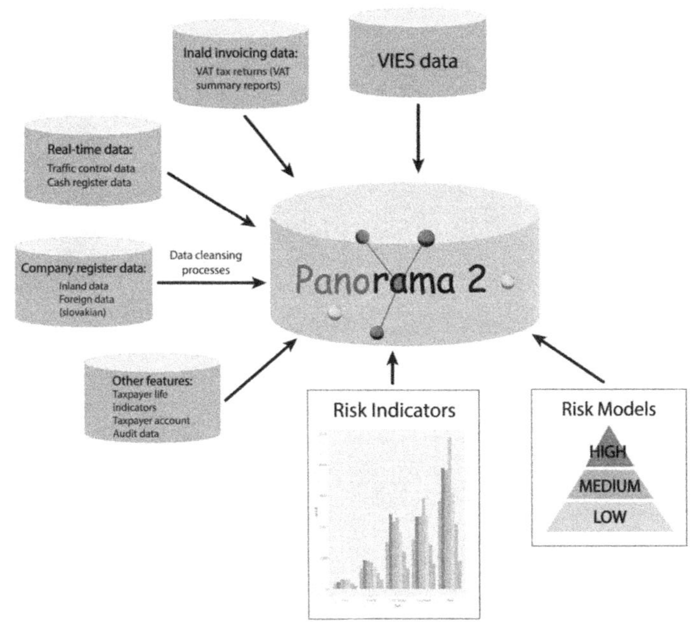

Risk indicators—Hierarchical clustering on declaration data	Usually, a risk indicator could be more complex. It could be an output of an advanced analytics model. For example: In Switzerland risk indicators are calculated on the basis of hierarchical clustering. *Figure 4.20 Hierarchical Clustering on Declaration Data* 

Risk indicators—Business rules	It aims at using rules defined by a business, as risk indicators. For example, it is prevalent in Switzerland, where business ideas are integrated and evaluated as new risk indicators.

Figure 4.21 Business Rules

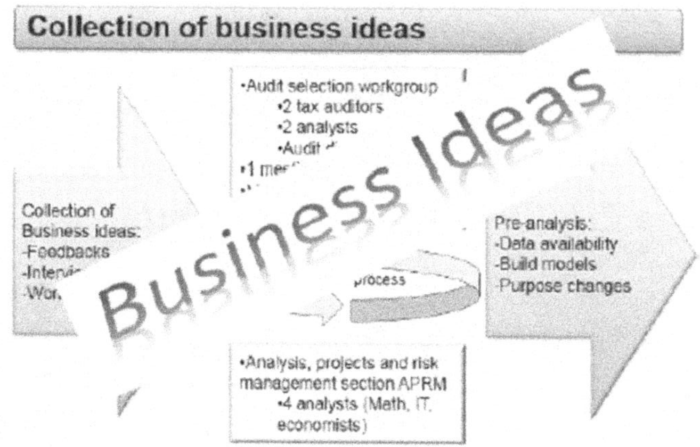

c. Data visualization

Visualizing complex taxpayer relationships and risk management results at the same time	Panorama visualization tool is a visualization tool that helps in finding satisfactory answers to many of the questions. It is designed to show different types of invoicing and hierarchy relations revealed by analyzing taxpayer networks. It also visualizes the rule-based risk assessment results, which is helpful for tax administrations.
Multifunctional system with data visualization functions	Same data can be used by different departments for different purposes. Considering this, the Spanish Tax administration has developed a multifunctional system called "Zujar." The tool provides visualized reports that can be generated with ease and can be used for different purposes. **Each department uses the same data sets for different purposes.**

Figure 4.22 The Spanish Zujar System

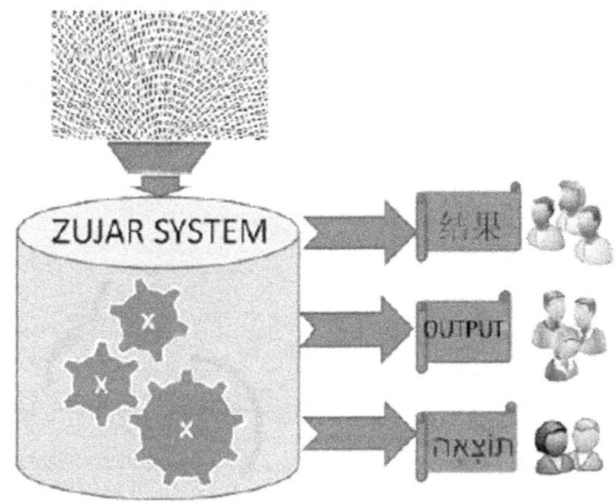

Transaction Network Analysis in the EU	Cross-border "carousel fraud" leads to leakage of VAT revenues. Under these techniques, automated data mining mechanics are applied to data provided by companies in their VAT returns, thereafter, networks are detected where fraudulent (trading) transactions occur.
Social network analysis for fraud detection	This technique is a useful tool for risk assessment. For example, the Spanish Tax Administration can derive information for any network through open-source tools by building and visualizing social networks.

Figure 4.23 Visualization of a Network of Taxpayers and Companies

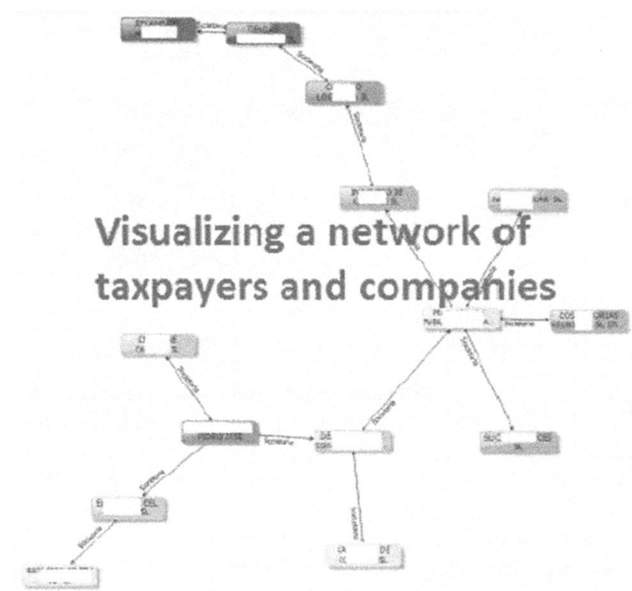

Note: The figure is available online at https://www.iota-tax.org/sites/default/files/pub/gpg_project/iota-practice-guide.pdf.

Even Enterprise-wide Social Network Analysis system is used by The Inland Revenue Authority of Singapore[34] to reflect the relationships between people, organizations and various entities. This enhances the risk profiling capability and decision-making.

34. OECD (2017), *The Changing Tax Compliance Environment and the Role of Audit*, OECD Publishing, Paris, https://doi.org/10.1787/9789264282186-en.

APPENDIX 2: A-H QUESTIONS RELATING TO THE THREE KEY IN-HOUSE ROLES AND RESPONSIBILITIES

Table 4.2 Questions A-G of the Three Key In-House Roles and Responsibilities

A	B	C	D	E	F	G
What is the governance on data?	Are there other any risk categories to be added?	What is your definition of clean data?	What are your categories of standards?	How deltas/risks are determined now?	Is there a materiality threshold?	Who are the relevant stakeholders?
Who is the supplier of data (tax team, finance team, etc.)?	Are these risk categories stable or volatile?	Will / can this clean data be used for other purposes?	Is there a hierarchy of standards?	Is there any process in place to determine deltas?	If yes, how do you apply the threshold?	Which reporting do these stakeholders expect?
What are the sources of data (ERP, Excel files, Word files, etc.)?	What is the weighting of risk categories?	Do you use a data manual / chart of accounts?	Are these standards subject to change?	Which deltas are tax-relevant?		What is the frequency of reporting?
What is the format of data (numbers, text, other)?	How do these risk categories fit into your "Enterprise Risk Management" (ERM)?					What is the format and the style of reporting?
What is the quality of data?						

Table 4.3 Questions H of the Three Key In-House Roles and Responsibilities

H. Regulatory and liability aspects
Is there any legal protection (e.g., attorney privilege)?
Is there a requirement / necessity for full disclosure of tax risk register?
What are the C-Suite liabilities in relation to disclosed information?
What is the governance on ERM / Tax risk management?

CHAPTER 5

Blockchain Tax Infrastructure: Building a Framework for Verified Tax Identity and Tax Document Management Exemplified by VAT Using Blockchain Technology

Robert Müller

1 INTRODUCTION

1.1 Setting the Scene

Globalization and digitization of the world are continuously increasing. Their rapid development, however, often causes cross-border tax issues that lead to difficulties in administration and assessment for taxpayers and tax administrations. To solve this, a transnational digital identity and document management system is required to enable taxable subjects and tax administrations to exchange documents with verified content and to uniquely identify taxpayers in cross-border situations. Trustworthy transmission of tax documents and the unique identification of taxpayers can be enabled by decentralized, tamper-proof blockchain technology. The new technical concept of self-sovereign identity makes it possible to establish a trustworthy verification of identities in multinational communication over the internet.

Tax administrations and taxpayers are already thinking globally. The success of legislative initiatives for the taxation of a global economy relies on an international perspective.[1] Further, questions regarding the digital economy have been confronting the tax community for several decades,[2] many of which relate to the international digitization and automation of tax law. Solutions for the international taxation of a digitized global economy must also be addressed by digitized tax administrations and taxpayers. These requirements do not currently receive the attention they should.[3]

Although we are seeing greater transparency in international taxation and the cross-border exchange of tax-relevant information,[4] this information is not yet bundled and concerns only individual data categories. Consequently, the automation and standardization of tax processes are challenging because independent data silos are created, and various data formats are used. Allocating and linking tax data, not to mention standardized cross-border communication between and with tax administrations, thus, becomes much more difficult.

The objective must, therefore, be to create a transnational system in which information can be transmitted securely, irrespective of the tax, the category of data, or other circumstances. In a digital world, the provenance of tax data is not always secure.

1. See in this context: OECD, *Addressing the tax challenges arising from the digitalisation of the economy*, https://www.oecd.org/tax/beps/brochure-addressing-the-tax-challenges-arising-from-the-digitalisation-of-the-economy-july-2021.pdf (accessed September 2, 2021).
2. In an early consideration: OECD, *Electronic Commerce: Taxation Framework Conditions* (1998).
3. See nevertheless in this context a thematic engagement that shows technological possibilities: OECD, *Technologies for Better Tax Administration—A Practical Guide for Revenue Bodies* (2016).
4. With a broad overview. In the meantime, transparency has increased further: X. Oberson, *International Exchange of Information in Tax Matters—Towards Global Transparency* (2015).

Conversely, tax authorities need trustworthy data and transparent processes from suitable sources for correct tax assessment and verification. This problem is not new. From a global perspective, the OECD regularly reiterates the potential of digital transformation, in tax administrations, to make voluntary compliance easier for taxpayers.[5] Additionally, any multinational system for the exchange of information will have to ensure that taxpayers' data is stored securely and transmitted only for the required purpose and with the taxpayer's consent.

Value added tax (VAT) is harmonized across Europe, and digital transformation is proceeding swiftly in several countries for important VAT functions, such as e-invoicing[6]. Given that VAT evasion is widespread, in cross-border situations, tax administrations have much to gain from transparent tax processes. This has led to strict compliance requirements for taxpayers in cross-border situations. They must comply with VAT obligations in a legally secure manner and prevent an emerging fragmentation of technical reporting requirements.[7] VAT, therefore, provides a suitable setting for the establishment of an appropriate transnational blockchain tax infrastructure (BTI) for identifying and exchanging tax documents.

1.2 The Investigation

Blockchain technology enables trustworthy communication on the internet and the establishment of sovereign identity and document management by the data holder. It potentially benefits not only tax administrations but also taxpayers, because the fulfilment of tax compliance requirements, as well as the efficiency and speed of tax processes, can be significantly improved. Numerous compliance software tools are currently available to taxpayers worldwide. Several blockchain applications[8] and a self-sovereign identity pilot[9] are already being developed for tax applications. To ensure interoperability between emerging and existing applications, a suitable framework is needed. The BTI concept could provide transnational interoperability, while ensuring the trustworthiness of identity verification and document management. The proposed concept is new and has not been implemented before, neither in an academic setting nor in practice. Regardless of the proposed technical implementation, however, it remains necessary to bundle and standardize data under international tax law.

5. OECD, *Tax Administration 3.0: The Digital Transformation of Tax Administration* 10 ff. (OECD 2020), http://www.oecd.org/tax/forum-on-tax-administration/publications-and-products/ (accessed September 20, 2021).
6. With an overview of countries and techniques used: N. Petrosino, *Are You Ready for the Tax Technology?*, IVM Volume 30 No. 2 (2019).
7. A. Kollmann, *Steuerliches "Massendaten-Reporting"—Ein Blick ins Ausland*, REthinking Tax, 53 ff. (2021).
8. See in this context for example: R. Risse/M. Gries, *Der Einsatz von Blockchain-Technologie in der Steuer- und Zollfunktion—Entwicklung eines ersten Anwendungsfalls: Langzeit- Lieferantenerklärungen*, beck.digitax, 388 ff. (2020); EY, *Withholding tax distributed ledger report*, https://assets.ey.com/content/dam/ey-sites/ey-com/en_gl/topics/tax/tax-pdfs/ey-withholding-tax-distributed-ledger-report.pdf (accessed August 13, 2021).
9. Based on the knowledge of the author: T. Guggenberger et al., *SSI@LfSt—Einsatz der Blockchain-Technologie in der Steuerverwaltung Projektgruppe Wirtschaftsinformatik des Fraunhofer-Instituts für Angewandte Informationstechnik FIT* (2020).

This chapter first analyzes the principles of the existing digital tax identity and document management. To a large extent, they are characterized by an internet user account-based approach. Existing challenges will be identified in this context. To solve these challenges, the self-sovereign identity concept using blockchain technology for implementation will be discussed and a technical explanation will be given. Afterwards, the concept of BTI based on a decentralized self-sovereign identity will be proposed. The key, decentralized identifiers and credential lifecycle are the backbones of the system. Rudimentary functions are the identification and communication between the network participants. The model has a generic structure and allows the modularization of tax use cases at the credential level. The implementation will be examined in a VAT context, taking into account current digital transformation developments in Europe. However, the actual implementation of BTI is largely dependent on the political environment and tax policy implementation.

In summary, the technology is available to harness the benefits of a globalized, digital world in taxation.

2 TECHNICAL BACKGROUND

2.1 Identity Management in a Globalized, Digital World

Central identity management is the key to many internet services; for example, website functions that are accessible only after entering a username and password. As a result, users can have multiple internet identities that are difficult to manage. This traps users because they do not have full control over the disclosed information, especially the duration and intensity[10] thereof.[11] In a conventional data sharing platform of this kind, data is held in specific domains of the service provider. This results in centralized control of data, either by companies or by governments.[12] This data is also outside the user's own data sphere, which means that handing over this data or forwarding and merging it is difficult. Another challenge is verifying information transmitted from trusted identities. User privacy is paramount; users must remain in possession of their own data and be able to be securely identified via identity and enter interactions with other parties. In summary, the traditional internet user environment involves a lack of data sovereignty for the user.[13]

This is also often the case with tax-related internet or reporting applications. Taxpayers register or verify their identity via the internet or another hybrid registration procedure and can subsequently use communication media or certain services. In cross-border situations, taxpayers often manage their data and tax identities separately

10. Thus, in an age query, the date of birth is decisive, although only the legal age limit is decisive, for example, whether a person is over 18 years.
11. Galia Kondova and Jörn Erbguth (eds.), *Self-Sovereign Identity on Public Blockchains and the GDPR* (2020).
12. H. Roßnagel et al., *Self-Sovereign and Decentralized Identity as the Future of Identity Management?* 37 f.
13. Rafael Belchior et al. (eds.), *SSIBAC: Self-Sovereign Identity Based Access Control* (2020).

for each jurisdiction.[14] This creates different tax data silos and data formats, making interoperability between jurisdictions difficult. Simultaneously, the legitimate exchange of data between tax administrations on cross-border issues is made more difficult. For the taxpayer, administrative acts take more time and resources. Tax processes can be more difficult to automate and providing a digital evaluation for tax purposes is problematic because data formats are not harmonized and tax documents need to be verified. This will not change unless taxpayers can be securely identified across borders and the exchanged data of tax documents can be securely transmitted in a verified manner.[15] It is, therefore, necessary to introduce more user-centric identities that are accepted across the various applications.

For several years, the self-sovereign identity (SSI) concept has been propagated to strengthen the data sovereignty of internet users. When using SSI systems, users retain complete ownership of their data and can present selected information directly to another participant. To harness the full potential of the more user-centric SSI approach, secure verification of information about identities and transmitted documents is particularly critical. This is where blockchain technology comes into play.[16] Blockchain elements are used only at necessary verification points.[17] Thereby, relevant data is not completely stored on a blockchain but merely anchored by allowing the content to be verified. In this context, the SSI topic is closely related to blockchain technology but is not based on it.[18] Blockchain technology supports the sovereign user data governance SSI concept through the properties of direct interactions between peers and decentralization.[19]

2.2 Blockchain Technology and Self-Sovereign Identity

2.2.1. Features of Blockchain Technology

As blockchain technology continues to mature, a blockchain ecosystem continues to develop.[20] A distributed ledger and decentralized interactions lie at the heart of blockchain technology. On a theoretical basis, every network participant can view all

---

14. Although individual Member States are already implementing uniform identities for tax applications and other e-government services, these do not yet exist for cross-border applications. However, these do not yet exist for cross-border applications. *See*, for example, Germany: A. Kowallik, *Integrierte Online-Plattformen der deutschsprachigen Finanzverwaltungen—Status quo, FinanzOnline und das neue deutsche Unternehmensportal*, beck.digitax, 155 f. (2020).
15. OECD, *supra* n. 5, at 45 f.
16. T. Ehrlich et al., *Self-Sovereign Identity als Grundlage für universell einsetzbare digitale Identitäten*, 58 HMD 2, 248 ff. (2021).
17. A. Giannopoulou/F. Wang, *Self-sovereign identity*, Internet Policy Review—Journal on internet regulation 2, 3 ff. (2021).
18. M. Cheesman, *Self-Sovereignty for Refugees? The Contested Horizons of Digital Identity*, Geopolitics, 6 ff. (2020).
19. Belchior et al. (eds.), *supra* n. 13, 1935.
20. Illustrated by the European maturity model of: G. Giaglis et al., *EU Blockchain Ecosystem Developments* (2020), https://www.eublockchainforum.eu/sites/default/files/reports/EU%20Blockchain%20Ecosystem%20Report_final_0.pdf (accessed July 19, 2021).

transactions and have full read and write permissions.[21] The technology in the original blockchain dogma avoids central parties that build trust in transmitted information. Instead, the blockchain technology builds trust by enabling parties to interact directly with each other over the internet.[22] Third parties are avoided by means of cryptographic encryption, which ensures maximum confidentiality, pseudonymity, and data integrity.[23] Hash values, which are mathematical puzzles, are generated for each transaction in a block and are interconnected to a chain.[24] Transaction manipulations can, thus, be detected more easily by the system. The immutability of this data ensures trust in the data stock, as well as the information transmitted. There are many deviations from these basic ideas of a permissionless public blockchain; for example, by means of a more centralized design, access restriction to the blockchain, or read and write permissions. Depending on the specific blockchain design, they are referred to as either permissioned public or permissioned private blockchains.[25] Transaction data must be validated by a consensus/validation mechanism of the network. A variety of consensus mechanisms have been designed.[26] For tax and more centralized applications, the proof-of-stake[27] or proof-of-authority[28] consensus mechanism is most suitable. It should be noted that although information can be stored in a blockchain in a tamper-proof manner, this does not guarantee that the information underlying the transaction has not itself been manipulated. This means that a blockchain does not protect against fake data, but only that data, once entered, is tamper-proof. This is what is known as the "oracle problem."[29]

As only limited data can be processed and stored on the blockchain and data protection problems can arise with data once it has been entered on the blockchain, a shift is underway to store only essential data for determining the truth of transactions on-chain. Other data remains off-chain and only elementary data for the verified transmission of the document and identity content; for example, the signature is stored on-chain.[30]

21. M. Iansiti/K.R. Lakhani, *The Truth about Blockchain*, Harvard Business Review, p. 125 (2017).
22. R.T. Ainsworth/A.B. Shact, *Blockchain Technology Might Solve VAT Fraud*, Tax Notes International, p. 1166 (2016).
23. J. Schrey/T. Thalhofer, *Rechtliche Aspekte der Blockchain*, NJW, 1431 f. (2017).
24. A. Bal, *Taxation, Virtual Currency and Blockchain* p. 10 (Kluwer Law International 2019).
25. K. Wüst/A. Gervais, *Do you Need a Blockchain?* Chapter: II. Background on Blockchain (IEEE Computer Society Conference Publishing Services ed., The Institute of Electrical and Electronics Engineers 2018).
26. I. Bashir, *Mastering Blockchain—Distributed ledgers, decentralization and smart contracts explained* 12, 13 f. (Packt Publishing 2017).
27. In proof-of-stake, a node is selected pseudo-randomly to validate the transaction: E. Filippova et al., *Blockchain: An Empirical Investigation of Its Scope for Improvement* p. 3 (J. Joshi et al. eds., Springer Nature Switzerland 2019).
28. A consensus mechanism for more restricted blockchain networks which relies heavily on the trustworthiness of individual validators.
29. R. Müller, *Kritische Bewertung des Blockchain-Hypes im Transfer Pricing*, Transfer Pricing International, 24 f. (2020).
30. R. Müller, *Das Blockchain-Framework Hyperledger im Steuerrecht—Entwicklung konkreter steuerlicher Blockchain-Anwendungen mit Hyperledger*, REthinking Tax 5, 11 f. (2021).

2.2.2. *Self-Sovereign Identity*

2.2.2.1 *General Properties*

No uniform SSI concept standard has yet been established. Technical blockchain-based SSI principles are in place, but several technical solutions have been developed that differ from each other.[31] In this chapter, an attempt is, therefore, made to obtain general statements and to demonstrate a technical framework, as well as to discuss the underlying potential for a modern identity/document management system in the area of taxation.

For better classification, different properties are attributed to SSI. Convincingly, Ferdous et al. summarize the following properties of SSI:[32]

- Foundational property
- Security property
- Controllability property
- Flexibility property
- Sustainability property

SSI initiatives are emerging in both the private and public sectors against a backdrop of growing interest in controlling identity information, as well as digital documents.[33] In its basic concept, SSI operates independently of central authorities, with complete autonomy and no external influences.[34] There is also no need to engage intermediaries to identify users by holding proof of identity. Identity data is not scattered across multiple applications or data silos but is centrally linked to the user/holder.[35] In contrast, there are other SSI concepts that have stronger governance structures and in which rights are controlled by central parties or the proof of identity is issued.[36] Not even anarchistic SSI ideas can manage without proof of identity because identity data must be provided by third parties.[37]

2.2.2.2 *Technical Terms*

In application-centric identity management, the user[38] must register and be authenticated separately for each application. A more user-centric SSI blockchain approach can

31. Kondova and Erbguth (eds.), *supra* n. 11, Chapter: 2 Self-Sovereign Identity.
32. M.S. Ferdous et al., *In Search of Self-Sovereign Identity Leveraging Blockchain Technology*, 7 IEEE Access, 103064 ff. (2019).
33. S. Mahula et al., "With blockchain or not? Opportunities and challenges of self-sovereign identity implementation in public administration" (DG.O'21: The 22nd Annual International Conference on Digital Government Research, Omaha NE USA, 2021), 495.
34. A. Satybaldy et al., *Self-Sovereign Identity Systems—Evaluation Framework* p. 3 (M. Friedewald et al. eds., 2019).
35. R. Belchior et al., *SSIBAC: Self-Sovereign Identity Based Access Control* 1935 f. (G. Wang et al. eds., 2020).
36. Roßnagel et al., *supra* n. 12, at p. 38.
37. Mahula, Tan and Crompvoets, *supra* n. 33, 496.
38. Or also referred to as holder.

ensure better interoperability, security, and privacy (*see* Figure 5.1). Trusted intermediaries are not necessary because a user can interact directly with service providers through its identity data. Information that is used to identify an individual is referred to as credentials. If this information can be verified, then verifiable credentials are available. The identity user receives these from a credential issuer.[39] The World Wide Web Consortium (W3C) has developed its own standards, known as Decentralized Identifiers (DIDs)[40] and Verifiable Credentials (VCs)[41]. DIDs have a uniform structure; only the method and the method-specific ID differ. The DID allows unique identification of a user without disclosing extensive non-essential identity information.[42] Users have wallets in which credentials or VCs can be stored.[43] In principle, credentials are all possible expressible states (tax documents, identity card information, grades, etc.). Credentials may contain information identifying the user. VCs enable verification via the verifiable presentation of the content using a digital signature. If an issuer issues a VC, verification is possible by checking the digital signature.

Figure 5.1 SSI Interactions[44]

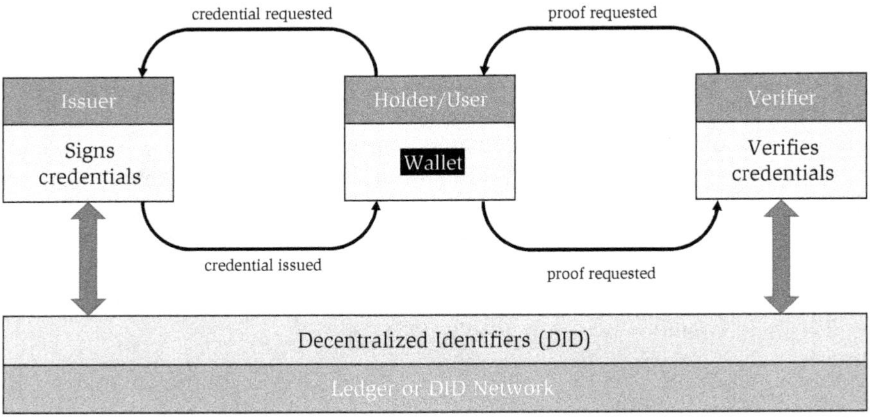

2.2.2.3 *What Are the Advantages and Disadvantages?*

The cryptographic implementation of hash values and public-private key pairs is not new. Advantages over a blockchain are the presence of a central instance, high scalability, and low latency of transactions. Disadvantages are the central identification of a user (via government agencies), the system being dependent on a higher-level

39. Roßnagel et al., *supra* n. 12, at 37, 38.
40. https://www.w3.org/TR/did-core/, accessed September 27, 2021.
41. https://www.w3.org/TR/vc-data-model/, accessed September 27, 2021.
42. Mahula et al., *supra* n. 33, 496.
43. See https://www.w3.org/TR/vc-data-model/#what-is-a-verifiable-credential (accessed September 27, 2021).
44. Adapted from: Mahula et al., *supra* n. 33, 496.

authority, which results in a single point of failure, and all users having to trust the decisions of the higher-level authority.[45] A potential SSI concept would be a hybrid between centralized and decentralized elements. A Trusted Accreditation Organization (TAO), such as a tax administration, would be a central superordinate entity and participants would have to trust it. A central authority for verifying identities and approving issuers would be a fundamentally antagonistic position to the decentralized blockchain philosophy. It makes sense, especially for identities in the SSI network, similar to the physical world, that government institutions link identity credentials securely to a network identity. This is already recognized in e-government SSI concepts and is supported in the literature.[46]

Likewise, the SSI concept need not be mandatorily linked to DIDs. It merely offers itself and was strongly propagated by the W3C.[47] From a standardization perspective, the initiative should be welcomed because it contributes to better interoperability of different systems.

3 IMPLEMENTING A EUROPEAN BTI

3.1 General System Requirements

The BTI is based on the SSI concept and is built in a generic way. The system focuses on identifying the taxpayer and the verified exchange of tax documents. Its infrastructure functions independently of use cases and is thus intended to form the basis for an emerging tax blockchain ecosystem. Potential use cases can leverage the credential level of the infrastructure to allow applications to be realized. If tax-relevant identities exist, potential can also be harnessed for other applications, for example, in auditing.

In the highly regulated tax field, such a system must be accepted by tax authorities. Tax documents could have an immediate tax effect as a VC for tax assessment purposes (e.g. invoices for input VAT or withholding tax documents for refunds). For this reason, issuer approval for VC issuance is a critical point.[48] Further, the admission to the system, as a holder of a VC, must be handled by a trusted authority. This trusted entity, which has a central position in rights management, is a TAO[49]: an entity with direct influence at critical governance stages in the otherwise autonomous execution of the lifecycle. In terms of tax policy, each TAO could be represented by a national tax administration or other organization of the relevant country. Another critical question is how TAOs will exercise rights management. In a global or at least European/transnational system, multiple tax authorities or authorized institutions would be represented as TAOs. These could form digital delegates,

45. W. Ertel/E. Löhmann, *Angewandte Kryptographie* 164 ff. (Carl Hanser 2018).
46. In this way: Mahula, Tan & Crompvoets, *supra* n. 33, 496, 497.
47. Cheesman, *supra* n. 18, at 6 f.
48. To this effect: Belchior et al., *supra* n. 35, at 1937.
49. Adapted from the European Blockchain Service Infrastructure Use-Case. However, only a Trusted Accreditation Registry (TAR) is mentioned. The central authority for managing this TAR is referred to as the TAO: https://ec.europa.eu/cefdigital/wiki/display/EBSIDOC/Diploma+Functional+Scope, accessed: August 27, 2021.

effectively voting majorities, to reach a consensus on the restriction or granting of rights. Blacklisting or whitelisting could also be introduced if, for example, issuers or holders are not trustworthy.

Likewise, trust must be established between the various and unknown parties in a multi-stakeholder process. The following minimum stakeholders are identified in the BTI:

- Trusted Accreditation Organization.
- Issuer.
- Holder.
- Requesting party.

The system is accessed by generating a key or subkey, which finally establishes a holder by means of a DID. Critical points are, therefore, the state "Create a key" and "Issuer signup via TAO." In addition to the generation of system access for relevant parties and the granting of certain read and write permissions, the degeneration of these rights is necessary. This applies to the issuer of a credential, the key generation, and the holder DID. To better illustrate a typical SSI lifecycle, the following distinction is made:

- Key lifecycle
- DID lifecycle
- Credential lifecycle

Each lifecycle basically operates separately from the others. The lifecycle border is crossed only once between the respective lifecycles.

Figure 5.2 Lifecycle of a Global Digital Tax ID Using Blockchain Technology

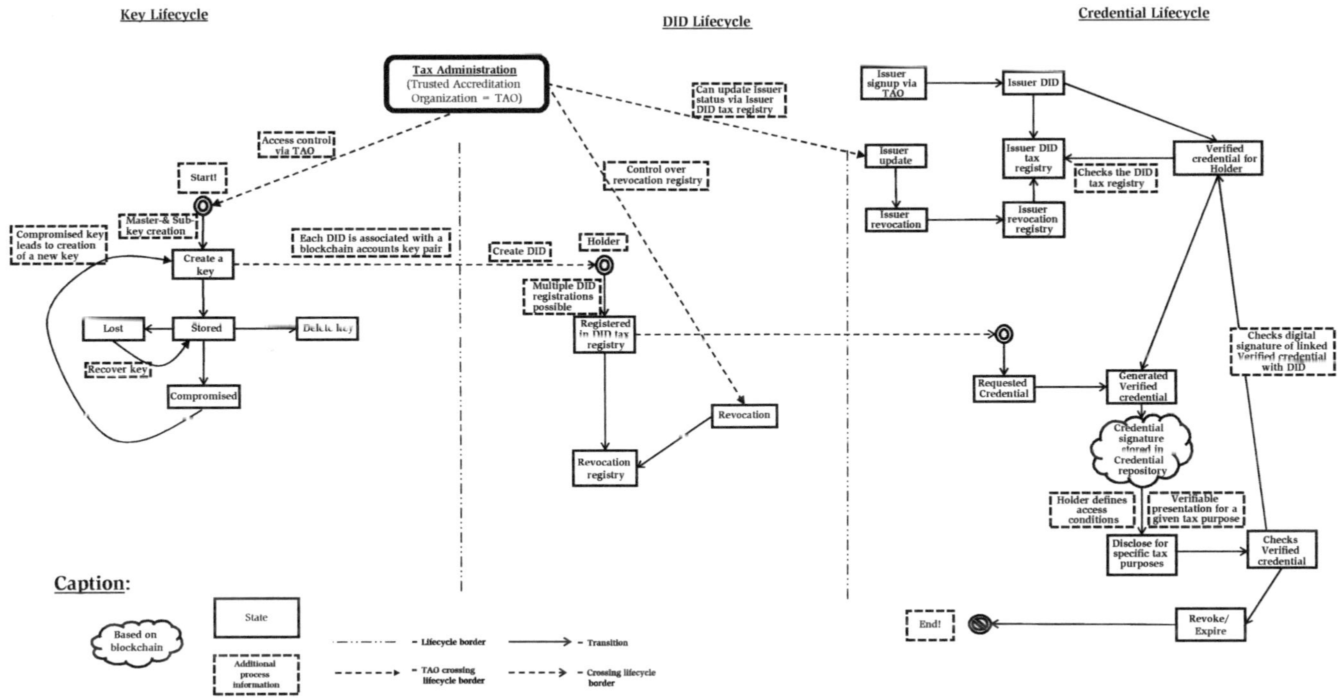

3.2 Lifecycle Explanations

3.2.1. Key Lifecycle

The key lifecycle starts with key access control for future users by the TAO. Alternatively, users could be uniquely identified by linking a DID to a DID document. However, this downstream approach does not make sense in a permissioned blockchain system, because a selection process can already take place at the key generation level for identification, as well as to prevent malicious attacks. Specifically, a key may be assigned by the relevant TAO (e.g., tax authority) for a taxpayer.

The TAO assigns a master key that can be used to manage subkeys. The subkeys can be used for different sub-identities; for example, for subsidiaries in a corporation. The literature also suggests using different subkeys for each new transaction via a new DID generation to ensure stronger privacy protection.[50] The master key is kept via public-private key management. If a user no longer exists or wants to end the use, it must also be possible to delete the key. At the same time, it must be possible to restore the key if it is lost; for example, the private key. If the master key is compromised, a new key must be created. To prevent key compromise, methods such as hot and cold wallets or splitting the keys (e.g., "key shards") are under discussion.[51]

3.2.2 DID Lifecycle

To generate a DID, it is linked to a blockchain account key pair. A DID can represent a holder for certain VCs. Since different subkeys can be generated, a separate DID can be assigned for each kind of tax (e.g., direct taxes, indirect taxes). This means that multiple DID registrations are theoretically possible. Holder DIDs are managed in a DID tax registry. If a DID enters into transactions or receives VCs, for instance, then a verification is performed to determine whether the DID is still up to date. TAOs, thus, gain control over the functions of DIDs. If, for example, a DID is not trusted or is no longer allowed to receive a VC, the TAO can enter a revocation in the revocation registry, which prevents the VC from being assigned to the DID in a verification. This renders the DID non-functional by the non-revocation proof.[52] Using this level, the VC can also no longer be associated with a DID. There are SSI concepts in which a DID is provided with an identity subject from an identity issuer. In principle, according to the W3C, a DID does not require a central authorization instance.[53] However, this is necessary in the current BTI case via the key assignment. An identity subject is assigned to the DID by the identity issuer (TAO) at an earlier level.

50. Y. Liu et al., "Design Patterns for Blockchain-based Self-Sovereign Identity" (EuroPLoP '20: European Conference on Pattern Languages of Programs 2020, Virtual Event Germany, 2020), Chapter: 3.1. Key Management Patterns.
51. *Ibid.*, Chapter: 3.1.2., 3.1.3.
52. Based on a German use case at the German tax authorities: Guggenberger et al., *supra* n. 9, at 28, 29.
53. Mahula, Tan & Crompvoets, *supra* n. 33, 496.

It is debatable whether the identifier associated with a DID document, to form a DID, should operate on-chain or off-chain. One proposal is to manage the identifier registry and identification data through a smart contract. The smart contract would be stored on-chain and the identifier data off-chain.[54] An application of this kind could sustain itself in a more permissionless public architecture. In fact, however, it is questionable whether the level of DID needs to be additionally secured via an on-chain/off-chain structure in an architecture that is restricted by TAOs.

3.2.3 *Modular Credential Lifecycle*

Many identity schemes and mechanisms have been proposed for a digital world in the last 20 years. None could prevail over application-centric approaches, because the digital ecosystem for sustainable business models and monetization has been absent.[55] Regardless of the proposed identity and document management system, it is critical that value is created for users and adopted by a broad base. Use cases must be developed that are important for identifying potential applications of blockchain technology in taxation, such as in VAT. However, network effects and an ecosystem only emerge with a larger-scale infrastructure. If globally trusted identities are available and verified document management and exchange can be ensured, then further use cases can be developed on the basis of this infrastructure. In the context of BTI, this occurs at the credential level.

The credential lifecycle is divided into two parts: the issuer level and the credential management. The issuer (e.g. a bank) first registers for the system via the TAO and receives an Issuer DID, which is entered in an Issuer DID tax registry. The issuer can now provide VCs to the holder. If the status of the issuer changes (e.g. because it has incorrectly issued VCs for the holder), the TAO can perform an issuer update and make an entry in the Issuer Revocation registry. The VCs created by the issuer are verifiable via a digital signature.

The credential signature is stored in the credential repository, which is on-chain. For the verifiable data registry to enable verifiable presentation, that is, verification of VCs, the data registry used must be decentral. In addition to the issued VC, a blockchain also documents the issuer of the VC. Therefore, a verifiable presentation of the VCs can be made to a third party (direct peer-to-peer communication) without the issuer having to take action.[56] The VC holder can define the access and scope of the VC. However, a tax impact potentially arising from the VC will, in practice, be linked by the tax authorities to certain tax-relevant information for verification. Thus, the taxpayer as the holder is free to decide how much and which information is shared from his VC, but for the occurrence of a tax impact, through the verified presentation of a VC, tax administrations or laws still determine the scope of the information to be disclosed. After the verified presentation, it is possible to revoke the VC or determine an expiration date for data access.

54. Liu et al., *supra* n. 50, Chapter: 3.2.1. Identifier Registry.
55. Roßnagel et al., *supra* n. 12, at 36, 37.
56. See similar architecture: Belchior et al., *supra* n. 35, at p. 1937.

The technical implementation of zero-knowledge proofs can ensure taxpayers' privacy and the integrity of tax documents in cross-border communication with tax authorities.[57]

VCs are not bound to specific content and can represent any tax document of a DID as a credential. Therefore, specific use cases can be implemented on the credential level. The mechanism for verifying VCs can also be used for other use cases.

3.2.4 Potential Tax Use Cases

3.2.4.1 General Remarks on Blockchain Tax Use Cases

The potential blockchain-based use cases are manifold for the tax sector. Applications can be considered especially in areas with a high transaction frequency and the need for verified transmitted information.[58] Use cases are considered in both direct and indirect taxation. For direct taxation, use cases in transfer pricing[59] and withholding tax[60] are particularly worth mentioning. In the field of indirect taxation, there are use cases for VAT[61] and customs[62]. The potential of transparent processes and trustworthy information is not restricted to tax authorities.[63] For taxpayers, tax-relevant data can be bundled and fed into an automated "real-time" audit.[64]

All use cases and the outlined applications have their justification in ensuring that the topic receives the necessary attention and that the potential of blockchain technology in tax law is recognized. From a global perspective, however, the use cases result in new data silos. The introduction of an interoperable structure is, therefore, desirable. A pilot project based on SSI technology has been developed in the German tax administration and was used in VAT for compliance functions in e-commerce.[65]

57. See in this context: F. Fatz et al., *Confidentiality-preserving Validation of Tax Documents on the Blockchain* (2020).
58. P. Fettke/R. Risse, *Blockchain: Wird eine sog. "real time" Tax Compliance möglich?*, DB, p. 1750 (2018).
59. R. Müller, *The Blockchain Technology in Transfer Pricing—Artificial Intelligence and Further Synergies*, International Transfer Pricing Journal (2020).
60. EY, *supra* n. 8.
61. R. Müller, *Blockchain und Smart Contract im Steuerrecht—Potenziale und Konzepte in der Mehrwertsteuer* (2020).
62. Risse/Gries, *supra* n. 8, at 391 f.
63. R. Müller, *'Automatisierte' Verrechnungspreisbestimmung - Entwurf eines Echtzeit-Horizontal-Monitoring mit Hilfe einer öffentlichen Blockchain*, WPg (2020).
64. With the perspective of an AI blockchain platform economy for automated assessment of tax-related issues: R. Müller, *Eine KI- und Blockchain-Plattformökonomie für das Steuerrecht*, Der Steuerberater (2021).
65. Guggenberger et al., *supra* n. 9.

It is becoming apparent that use cases and applications could be developed in VAT, especially for combating VAT fraud. Blockchain use cases in VAT can roughly be divided into three categories:

- Recording of trusted/verified transaction and invoice data.[66]
- Automated VAT collection.[67]
- Introduction of a VAT token (VATCoin).[68]

In transaction chains for VAT evasion, uninvolved companies ("buffers") can be used to disguise criminal structures.[69] The traceability of transaction chains can be useful in uncovering these structures. This can be achieved in a tamper-proof manner by tracking relevant data on blockchain elements. The EU Commission is already evaluating the potential of blockchain technology in VAT.[70] VAT evasion is high in Europe, and VAT compliance requirements are challenging for taxpayers. The digitization of VAT processes through private state cooperation has already been demonstrated in the People's Republic of China. To combat carousel fraud, blockchain-based e-invoices have been recorded in Shenzhen, since 2016.[71] This also offers the potential for taxable persons to meet their VAT compliance obligations more easily. Hence, there is a need to transform VAT processes in Europe for a digitized, automated future with the help of blockchain technology.[72]

3.2.4.2 *VAT and Digitization of Functions*

3.2.4.2.1 Introduction

Fundamental for all blockchain use cases in VAT is the recording of VAT-relevant information; that is, invoice data and transaction data. Independent of the use case, VAT-relevant information, therefore, provides the basis for digitization through a blockchain. Once recorded, VAT-relevant data would not be corruptible and would, therefore, be trustworthy. Since VAT functions are currently being digitized in several European countries, a comparison with these developments is useful for transferring principles to the BTI. In Europe, there are two basic system approaches to the digitizing of VAT functions. In the clearance model, the e-invoice is issued to the invoice recipient via a central tax administration system after automated invoice verification. In reporting models, readable formats are transferred non-automatically to the tax

66. F. Fatz et al., *Potenziale von Blockchain-Anwendungen im Steuerbereich*, HMD Praxis der Wirtschaftsinformatik, 1236 ff. (2018).
67. For instance: R. Müller, *Proposal for an Automated Real-Time VAT Collection Mechanism in B2C E-Commerce using Blockchain Technology*, IVM Volume 31, No. 3 (2020).
68. See in this regard the following fundamental paper: Ainsworth/Shact, *supra* n. 22, at 1165 ff.
69. C.S. Ruiz, *How Criminals Evade VAT and How We Use New Techniques to Detect It*, ECA Journal No. 2 (2019).
70. S. Paez, *EU Developing Technology for Better Tax Information Sharing*, Tax Notes International, p. 1239 (2021).
71. R. Müller, *Blockchain Applications in Asian Tax Administrations*, APTB 2020 Vol 26 No. 2, Chapter: Blockchain Application in PRC.
72. R. Müller, *Building a Blockchain for the EU VAT*, Tax Notes International, 1044 ff. (2020).

authorities at varying times. The data is structured, using Spain as an example, and is transmitted in an XML file.[73] These approaches are tax administration-centric, alongside digitization initiatives, by entrepreneurs, to better comply with VAT obligations.[74] One driver in digitizing VAT is e-commerce, which is frequently set up across borders. Digitizing VAT functions in this context is increasingly necessary to avoid regulatory barriers to economic growth.[75]

3.2.4.2.2 Important Digitization Developments in Europe

EU Directive 2014/55/EU[76] contains an obligation to issue electronic invoices to a contracting public authority (business-to-government, or B2G). The directive requires public authorities to accept and process issued structured e-invoices. As an interesting implementation example, Italy started expanding an electronic invoicing clearance system in January 2019. This permission was granted, to Italy, on April 16, 2018, by the EU Commission, in accordance with Articles 218, 232 of Council Directive 2006/112/EC (VAT Directive)[77]. The *Sistema di Interscambio* (SdI) applies to both business-to-business (B2B) and business-to-consumer (B2C) situations.[78] In addition to being issued in electronic form, invoices are also transmitted between the parties involved via the central SdI system operated by the Italian tax authorities. As a consequence, the invoice is transmitted in a standardized format and can subsequently be processed automatically. The entrepreneur must transmit the invoice via the SdI; otherwise, the invoice recipient cannot claim an input tax refund. When the invoice is forwarded to the recipient, mandatory fields, such as the VAT identification number, are identified.[79] From the beginning of 2022, invoices from and to non-resident entrepreneurs will also be reported to the tax authorities, at the end of the month. Advantageously, a taxpayer's invoices can also be stored free of charge by the tax authorities, fulfilling the documentation compliance requirements.[80] France plans to introduce a similar clearance approach in VAT, from 2023. In contrast to Italy, invoices can also be exchanged between entrepreneurs in previous formats via certified service

73. Petrosino, *supra* n. 6, at Chapter 2. SAF-T Reporting in the European Union: Analysis.
74. B. Kuijper et al., *Technology-Enabled Tax Compliance,* Bulletin for International Taxation, p. 590 (2020).
75. Illustrates regulatory barriers: A.-K. Heidbüchel/R. Gothmann, *Warum die Umsatzsteuer das Wachstum der digitalen Gatekeeper aktuell und zukünftig bremsen könnte,* REthinking Tax 5, 39 ff. (2021).
76. Directive 2014/55/EU of the European Parliament and of the Council of 16 April 2014 on electronic invoicing in public procurement, OJ L 133/1.
77. Council Directive 2006/112/EC of 28 November 2006 on the common system of value added tax, OJ L 347/1.
78. Agenzia Entrate, *La fattura elettronica e i servizi gratuiti dell'agenzia delle entrate,* aggiornata al 4 ottobre 2018, S. 2. https://www.agenziaentrate.gov.it/portale/documents/20143/451290/guida + FE + e + servizi + AdE + in + pdf_Guida_La + fattura_elettronica_e_i_servizi_g_1008202 0.pdf/035e38b3-2309-3335-f135-6e6010252e7a (accessed October 13, 2021).
79. A. Bal, *VAT Trends in Europe: Digitalization and Real-Time Filing,* Tax Notes International, 721 f. (2019).
80. A. Kollmann, *Heterogenes nationales Steuerreporting - Eine Herausforderung für multinationale Unternehmen,* beck.digitax 3, p. 210 (2021).

providers. However, the transmission of relevant VAT data to the tax authorities is mandatory.[81]

In contrast, Spanish companies must perform almost "real-time" reporting; that is, invoices, also with a cross-border background, must be transmitted to the tax authorities within a short period of time.[82] Unlike clearance models, real-time reporting approaches do not generate synergy effects through the standardization of formats, and the further processing of documents by machines is made more difficult. At the same time, real-time reporting imposes fewer requirements in comparison, because VAT processes do not have to be digitized from scratch. As a result, implementing a clearance model is likely to be more complex, but stronger synergy effects may result from the complete machine usability of e-invoice information. In addition to the automated processing of invoice information and a more automation-friendly document flow through standardized data formats, synergy effects also result; for example, in a smaller ecological footprint through fewer paper invoices, less VAT evasion, better verification of other types of taxes, and improved automated auditability by auditors or tax advisors.

3.2.4.2.3 Findings for the BTI

There is, thus, a clear preference for digitizing VAT information via a clearance system. This also applies to the technical implementation in a blockchain-based system. To counteract the emerging technical fragmentation of VAT infrastructures in Europe, it would be desirable to introduce mandatory harmonized e-invoicing at the European legal level. A legal framework for the mandatory introduction of e-invoicing can be introduced in the EU through a proposal by the EU Commission, if all member states agree, according to Article 395 (1) VAT Directive. Modifications pursuant to Articles 218 and 232 VAT Directive would be necessary for the introduction of European clearance e-invoicing.[83] At the technical level, a harmonized solution is also advisable. This should be done in Europe by introducing a regulation, because this would set binding standards for all member states. Given that VAT is one of the most harmonized types of tax in Europe, the introduction of BTI lends itself via VAT functions. In Europe, cross-border transactions occur frequently, due to intra-community supplies under Article 138 VAT Directive. In addition to a blockchain-based mandatory recording of national invoices in B2B transactions, the next logical development step of BTI is, therefore, in cross-border situations. Based on a BTI implementation of VAT processes, other tax types can also be integrated, such as withholding tax, customs, or transfer pricing. Related to VAT, invoices can be presented as VCs by the invoicing party. The invoice recipient can present the VC to the tax authorities to receive an input tax

81. Kollmann, *supra* n. 7, at 57, 58.
82. Petrosino, *supra* n. 6, at Chapter 2.3. SII in Spain.
83. Wissenschaftliche Dienste, *Sachstand: Möglichkeiten zur Einführung eines E-Rechnungs- und Clearance-Verfahrens in Deutschland* Chapter 4. Unionsrechtlicher Rahmen für die Ermächtigung zur Einführug einer verpflichtenden elektronischen Rechnung (Art. 395 Abs. 1 MwSt-SystRL) (2021).

refund. In intra-community supplies, documentation requirements and verification by the tax authorities can also be carried out via a verified presentation.

4. DISCUSSION

In conclusion, the question is whether blockchain technology and the SSI-based BTI, on the one hand, or more traditional applications on the other, are more suitable for implementing digitized tax functions. Here, the focus must be on a wider global context. Although, as explained above, clearance systems in VAT can already be implemented with traditional non-blockchain-based solutions, the full potential of a cross-border tax identity and document management system goes beyond this use case. Validating documents and identifying network participants is not use case-specific and is particularly suitable for cross-border tax situations. The BTI is not limited to taxpayer-tax administration situations. Rather, overall tax processes with relevant stakeholders can be accelerated (e.g. financial institutions issuing tax certificates to taxpayers). Potential emerges in the tax verification of transmitted information and the network participants involved. This can also be relevant for tax advisors or auditors. The BTI must, therefore, be understood as a global communication infrastructure, where taxpayers and tax administrations can work together within the framework of efficient horizontal monitoring.

5. SUMMARY

Identity and document management, in a digital and global tax world, must be built on new infrastructures operating across borders. To create a solid framework, infrastructures must be established in which unknown parties (taxpayers, tax administrations, etc.) can exchange digital documents with each other in a trustworthy manner, via a single point. This is also essential from an administrative perspective because only in this way can the ever-increasing internationalization of taxes be managed electronically, in a meaningful way.

These infrastructures can be handled via a blockchain-based self-sovereign identity management system, as demonstrated. It not only guarantees the secure identification of network participants, but also contributes to the digitization of tax information. At the same time, confidentiality of sensitive tax data can be better guaranteed, thus, providing greater protection against a "transparent" taxpayer and the disclosure of sensitive tax data via unauthorized access. It is advisable to start integrating VAT processes into the BTI in Europe, because basic VAT data could easily be digitized, and the legal framework is harmonized across borders. This would also combat an emerging or already existing technical fragmentation of tax reporting systems and simultaneously create synergy effects for a more effective automation of tax processes.

A further benefit is greater legal certainty for taxpayers and tax administrations, because the auditing of tax processes can be achieved earlier and—by automation—more efficiently.

CHAPTER 6

Process Mining for Tax and Customs-Related Processes: How to Introduce Concrete Use Cases?

Robert Risse

1 INTRODUCTION

Process mining is a young discipline. To explain it simply, it is a data-based process management approach. The benefits and potentials, associated with this process management approach, are recognized in organizations of all sizes.[1] There has been a steady increase in global awareness, of this young management discipline, since the launch of the Process Mining Manifesto, by leading academic experts, in 2011.[2] Organizations that have already implemented process mining tools report unprecedented knowledge about their process landscape.[3] But how are such remarkable results achieved? This chapter will take a closer look at the basic principles of process mining (section 2), and then apply these principles to tax compliance use cases (section 3). Furthermore, a system of tax compliance testing based on process mining will be described. Process mining is well suited for future tax audits in the context of a cooperative compliance approach (section 4). Finally, the possibilities of auditing tax processes through the process mining techniques are summarized and evaluated (section 5).

2 PRINCIPLES OF PROCESS MINING

In the age of Big Data, organizations rely on various information systems to perform individual process steps. Be it an Enterprise Resource Planning (ERP) system for tracking production processes, or a Customer Relationship Management (CRM) system for coordinating sales and customer service processes.[4] Nowadays, there is hardly a process that is not supported by at least one IT system. These systems continuously collect large amounts of data. Every order or delivery of goods or services leads to a digital footprint of the respective business process. This development makes process mining interesting for tax processes and relevant tax compliance. The Dutch tax authorities have already used process mining to conduct initial investigations of tax processes as part of the Dutch so-called horizontal monitoring program.[5]

1. Marlon Dumas, Marcello La Rosa, Jan Mendling, Hajo A. Reijers, Fundamentals of Business Process Management, 2nd edition, 2018, p. 1; Lars Reinkemeyer, Process Mining in Action, 2020, p. 3.
2. Gehrke, N., Müller-Wickop, N., 2010. Basic principles of financial process mining a journey through financial data in accounting information systems. In. Proceedings of the 16th Americas Conference on Information Systems, 10th; van der Aalst, H., Leopold, H., Reijers, H.A., 2015. Detecting inconsistencies between process models and textual descriptions. In: Motahari-Nezhad, H.R., Recker, J., Weidlich, M. (Eds.), Business Process Management: 13th International Conference, BPM 2015, Innsbruck, Austria, August 31–September 3, 2015, Proceedings. Springer International Publishing, Cham, pp. 90–105. van der Aalst, W.M.P., 2016. Process Mining: Data Science in Action; van der Aalst, W.M.P., Buijs, J., Van Dongen, B., 2012. Towards improving the representational bias of process mining. In: Data-driven Process Discovery and Analysis, pp. 39–54. van der Aalst, W.M.P., de Beer, H.T., van Dongen, B.F., 2005. Process Mining and Verification of Properties: An Approach Based on Temporal Logic. In: Springer Berlin Heidelberg, Berlin, Heidelberg, pp. 130–147.van der Aalst, W.M.P., Dongen, B.F.v., Herbst, J., Maruster, L., Schimm, G., Weijters, A.J.M.M., 2003. Workflow mining: a survey of issues and approaches. Data Knowl. Eng. 47 (2), 237–267. van der Aalst, W.M.P., van Hee, K.M., van der Werf, J.M., Verdonk, M., 2010. Auditing 2.0: using process mining to support tomorrow's auditor. Computer 43 (3), 90–93. van der Aalst, W.M.P., Weijters, T., Maruster, L., 2004. Workflow mining: discovering process models from event logs. IEEE Trans. Knowl. Data Eng. 16 (9), 1128–1142.
3. Lars Reinkemeyer, Process Mining in Action,2020, p. 1.
4. Lars Reinkemeyer, Process Mining in Action,2020, p. 3.
5. Process Mining at the Dutch Tax Office, available: https://fluxicon.com/camp/2012/5, 8.8.2021.

In a typical organization, several thousand business events are recorded everyday, in an ERP system. This results in valuable information; that is, process management information, which can be used and evaluated. This is where process mining comes into play. It uses the data collected by IT systems, the so-called event logs as data about data as so-called metadata.[6] The metadata enables deeper process analysis. Unlike more traditional business intelligence approaches, process mining not only uncovers problems, but also allows the user to find out "why" something went wrong in the process. Using process mining tools, organizations can move from a "trust-based" approach to a "data-driven" approach. Optimization measures can be taken based on real-time data by using Process Mining. Process Mining enables organizations to monitor, analyze and improve their actual processes with microscopic precision. Moreover, actual process execution is revealed with ease and an organization can keep track of key KPIs. Process Mining can be divided into various techniques:[7]

Technique 1 is an automatic process recognition. This uses the log files described above to autonomously design a process model with the help of artificial intelligence. This reconstruction of the actual model contributes to a fact-based understanding of the process flow, and forms the basis for any further analysis. In addition, the new process model can also map the underlying social network and show all resources involved in the different process steps.

Technique 2 is a technique that involves conformance checks. It uses the model created by process recognition and checks its conformance with a given set of rules. The goal is to verify that the process recorded in the event log conforms to a prescribed or expected behavior, such as a specific process model or written compliance rules. A common example of such a compliance rule is the "four-eyes principle", which is often used in procurement processes and also in the tax return preparation processes.

Technique 3 is when process mining software allows the company to easily compare two or more variants of a business process. Thus, variant analysis is performed. For this purpose, the event log is divided into several smaller event logs. One event log usually contains all the cases that led to a positive result. The second event log contains the cases that had a negative outcome. In this way, companies can analyze the differences in workflows in detail and derive data-driven suggestions for improvement.

Technique 4 is when there is the option for performance mining. This technique extracts a set of statistics about process performance to provide a deeper understanding about the underlying process. The result is a process model that clearly highlights bottlenecks, rework, waiting times, and process loops, thus, revealing previously hidden inefficiencies throughout the process flow.

6. Lars Reinkemeyer, Process Mining in Action,2020, pp. 3 ff.
7. Michael Werner, Financial process mining-Accounting data structure dependent control flow inference, International Accounting Information Systems 2017 available: http://dx.doi.org/10.1016/j.accinf.2017.03.004.

Now that the "what" process mining is and how it is performed has been addressed, it is important to clarify the "why"; that is, why should this technology be implemented? There are numerous reasons and use cases for using a process mining solution. Overall, the use of such a solution creates tremendous transparency for the processes under investigation. Companies and organizations can monitor their KPIs, as well as check process compliance. Thanks to this know-how, it provides operational support to make better process-related decisions and redefine target processes. Regardless of whether organizations already have an established business process management or are just starting with process management or digital transformation, process mining can optimally accompany process management. In particular, thanks to automated business process recognition, it can open up a fast entry into BPM (business process management). In addition, it enables companies to completely capture processes and, therefore, supports many digitization projects, such as:

- Implement a continuous process improvement cycle, understanding real end-to-end processes and introducing optimization measures based on real-time data. Tax compliance review is one of the essential elements of the Dutch tax authority's process mining pilot.[8]
- Improve process efficiency, analyze bottlenecks, process loops, and duplicate work that would otherwise go undetected.
- Identify, through the Business Process Discovery phase, the business processes that are more efficient than the "standard."
- Improve customer satisfaction, in the tax area to improve the tax compliance level.
- Support GRC management. Compliance testing to analyze if processes are compliant with all required rules and regulations and the identification of non-compliant cases. In tax law, risk management goes hand in hand with potential violation of tax law regulations. Compliance auditing supports error prevention and, thus, the essential element of risk management, the avoidance of risk through appropriate countermeasures.
- Implement Digital Process Automation/RPA. Recognizing opportunities for Robotic Process Automation to accelerate automation projects. The combination of the techniques of Process Mining with an RPA is an essential element for the automation of fiscal processes.[9]

8. Process Mining at the Dutch Tax Office, available: https://fluxicon.com/camp/2012/5, 8.8.2021, Charts 11: *The "new kind of auditing" by analyzing the process with a process mining tool gives the auditor a complete view on all the weaknesses in a process. The auditor has more detailed information about the quality of the processing of transactions and can give a better advice to improve processes or organizations.*
9. Jerome Geyer-Klingeberg, Janina Nakladal, Fabian Baldauf, Fabian Veit, rocess Mining and Robotic Process Automation: A Perfect Match, available: https://www.researchgate.net/profile/Jerome-Geyer-Klingeberg/publication/326466901_Process_Mining_and_Robotic_Process_Automation_A_Perfect_Match/links/5b4f787ea6fdcc8dae2b378c/Process-Mining-and-Robotic-Process-Automation-A-Perfect-Match.pdf, 8.8.2021.

In summary, the basic prerequisite of process mining is the existence of event logs from different systems. From this arise the process mining [10] functions of the following:

Discover

- Enables the visualization of processes.
- Points out and makes actual visible processes.
- Records for process documentation.
- Identifies all process variations, deviations, inefficient points and their origin.
- Provides transparency in the actual processes and shows deviations from the assumed actual processes or target design.

Conformance Checking/Monitoring

- Supports compliance.
- Enables the comparison of own actual processes with the benchmark of the defined target processes.
- Monitors the actual process execution.
- Identifies occurring compliance deviations.
- Prerequisites: Process mining in regular operation.

Enhancement

- Analysis of the process model.
- Improvement of the process model in terms of process optimization.
- Identification and documentation of tax-relevant processes (creation of transparency. Examples: Initial process mapping to create a process pool (as a basis for Tax Compliance Management Systems)., CMS).[11]
- Validation of target versus actual process.
- Automation and process control by process mining (conformance checking/monitoring).

Examples: Permanent validation (e.g., real-time) as part of Tax CMS regular operations.

- Implementation of migration path to mitigate process breaks and risks.
- Application of Process Mining makes sense for processes that are run through frequently, involve many actors, have a certain basic structure, and have a high compliance risk.

10. Van der Aalst, Process Mining: Overview and Opportunities, ACM Transactions on Management Information Systems, Vol.99, Article 99, 2012.
11. OECD paper: Co-operative Tax Compliance, Building Better Tax Control Frameworks, available: https://www.oecd.org/publications/co-operative-tax-compliance-9789264253384-en.htm, 8.8. 2021.

Example: tax reporting processes or any operational business processes that have a tax or customs relevance (order-to-cash, purchase-to-pay, ship to or ship from processes).

Process mining and data analytics should also be used in combination, for instance, for the tracking of subsequent changes to documents in ERP, for example, SAP-FI module after checking and submitting of advance VAT return.

3 PROCESS MINING IN TAX-RELEVANT PROCESSES

Operational processes in a company are characterized by events, a typical business transaction which results in various processing steps. A customer inquiry triggers the creation of a quotation, which in turn can result in a customer order in a second step. In today's system landscape, operational processes leave behind the described multitude of data traces. An ideal example is a workflow management system, whose log files show when a particular case was started: which agent performed which tasks in which role, and when the case was closed again.

There are many other systems in which data traces can be searched. For example, in ERP systems, individual systems, e-mail systems and other application systems. All this data can be used to gain transparency about system behavior and to drive various further analyses.

Even processes and structures within operational organizations, such as the tax department, are not immediately perceptible at first. An essential tool for imaging analysis is the modeling of operational processes (*see* Figure 6.1), if possible with the help of the Business Process Modeling Notation (BPMN) or other comparable methods. However, while classic modeling approaches have the disadvantage that they often do not represent the actual, but idealized or non-real processes in the company, visualization via process mining techniques make it possible to make the actual processes in the company visible and, thus, designable.

Figure 6.1 Typical Operational Process in Purchasing

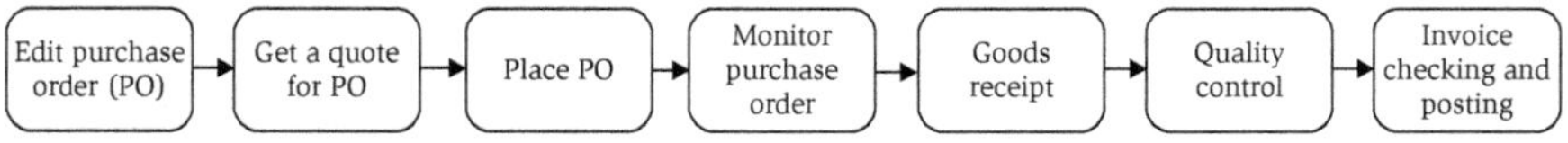

If Figure 6.1 is projected onto the control function, the data traces of the relevant IT systems corresponding to the control process flows will be used and systematically processed for visualization. The ideal typical point of connection is, thus, formed by classic workflow systems with activity log or even audit trail functionality. However, there is a wealth of other systems in the control function that can be used for fiscal process mining; for example: Enterprise Resource Planning (ERP); Supply Chain Management (SCM); Customer Relationship Management (CRM); Document Management System (DMS); custom application; and other upstream and downstream systems where traces of tax-related process activity can be found.

In addition to creating transparency, the examination of compliance issues in tax-relevant processes, in particular, has a high potential: the uncovered real process flow (de-facto process model) can be compared with the legally required flow (de-jure process model) and analyzed automatically with regard to deviations. Process mining is used to make tax-relevant processes visible. Processes that are run through frequently are particularly suitable for this purpose. Many actors should be involved in these processes. At the same time, the basic structure of the process has exceptions or other special features that need to be considered.

Value Added Tax (VAT): The process of an order via goods receipt, invoice receipt, tax invoice verification and payment of sales tax; that is, VAT after a tax return that has been prepared will regularly be accessible to a process mining analysis. The same applies to the sales process and the associated tax obligations.

Customs: The movement of goods during import and export for purchases, sales, intra-company movement of goods, between affiliated companies, provide interesting starting points for analysis. In particular, the combination between the sales tax and customs processes, which leads to new insights into the quality of the processes. Is import VAT booked as a cost or claimed as input VAT? In customs processes, such as for the use of free trade agreements (FTA), the question is whether all requirements for an FTA are met. The master data and process quality are, thus, crucial for significant cost savings. These are questions that are explored with process mining.

Transfer pricing: Operational support for the determination and documentation of transfer prices offers starting points for analysis with process mining. In order to determine the correct transfer price, various tasks, documentation and calculations must be performed. Typical transfer pricing process questions can be in this context: Are transfer prices accurately reflected by the associated companies? Do the desired income tax consequences for, for example, corporate income tax occur? Has a change in transfer pricing also led to a change in the transactional customs value, and has this caused the change in the VAT tax base? Does the chosen transfer price correspond to the transactional customs value? What happens if discrepancies are found between these values?

Payroll tax: Various processes that are present when an employee enters or leaves the company, when carrying out payroll, travel expense reimbursements, or other related activities, such as carrying out the taxation of non-cash fringe benefits for participation in events or hospitality, can provide starting points for an accurate tax recording.

Excise taxes: The processes of maintaining inventory, putting into and taking out of tax warehouses, and the like, may be of interest. How are excisable materials used, for production, laboratories, or other facilities? Depending on the consumption occasion there may be different tax consequences. For example, where is the self-generated electricity delivered? If it is to the production, it is immediately tax-exempt or if it is to the vending machines, then it is taxable. How does the combination with important processes, from other company functions, operate? The electricity tax can be reduced, in Germany, according to the law, among other things, to relieve the pension insurance contributions. For the calculation, the employer's pension insurance contribution payments are deducted from the electricity tax payments, according to a formula. A correct determination of the pension insurance contributions and payments is, therefore, necessary to be able to pay a correct electricity tax. This combination of processes has a direct monetary impact if process parts are not calculated and presented correctly.

4 TAX COMPLIANCE AUDIT PROCEDURES

A tax or customs compliance review process is both a data mining and process mining techniques model. An active improvement approach is used to review, as well as continuously improve fiscal compliance. The main contributions to the compliance system are:

- The algorithm: the transactions to be examined are classified into "OK" or "Not OK." Not all transactions are to be classified into these two classes. The algorithm must be trained for continuous improvement based on real data and process flows, so-called supervised learning. This requires a tax and customs expert to be involved in the data mining approach. The classifier algorithm is trained by the expert with new information in order to classify special cases classified as "Not OK" into the "OK" category as far as possible in the future.
- The internal control test task, itself, is represented as a generic process in the BPMN specifications. An overview of the business processes and their implementation, in the current state, enables companies to identify potential improvements.

Internal control testing is a verification process that corresponds to the first level of continuous assurance of process flows and analytical monitoring, as a transactional verification.

How transactional verification is performed is presented using the generic process of internal control testing. The purchasing process as depicted in Figure 6.1, and abstracts the level of automation that is applied. In this way, the core process of internal control testing is presented, regardless of the maturity level of continuous testing.

- However, the process assumes a contemporary financial reporting environment in which information systems, such as enterprise resource planning (ERP) systems are used. It also takes the exception-based principle of continuous audit as its foundation. This generic process overview facilitates the identification of opportunities to use analytics for transaction verification.

The following tax compliance audit model evolves from the above principles.

4.1 First Step of the Test: BPMN[12]

Once a business process has been selected for testing its associated internal controls, the first step is to gain a general understanding of the process. An essential challenge in process mining is this fundamental step of the creation of useful process models. First, the process models are often seen as too complex for simple interpretation and analysis. Extremely complex models are referred to as *spaghetti processes* (*see* Figure 6.2) in the process mining community due to their graphical characteristics of intertwined arcs in the respective process models.[13]

Figure 6.2 Representation of Existing Enterprise Processes with Process Mining Without Detailing

However, the purpose of the first step in using BPM is to understand the process that serves as the normative process. This understanding can be gained through document review, interviews, previous experience with the company, and so on. Many companies have also had experience with processes in shared service centers (SSC). The next step is for further automation of these processes harmonized in the SSC. The combination of process mining and RPA shows the considerable potential of RPA performance measurement.[14]

12. Marlon Dumas, Marcello La Rosa, Jan Mendling, Hajo A. Reijers, Fundamentals of Business Process Management, 2nd edition, 2018.
13. Van der Aalst, 2011b, Michael Werner, Financial process mining-Accounting data structure dependent control flow inference. In: International Journal of Accounting Information Systems, p. 57-80, available: http://dx.doi.org/10.1016/j.accinf.2017.03.004.
14. Jerome Geyer-Klingeberg, Janina Nakladal, Fabian Baldauf, Fabian Veit, rocess Mining and Robotic Process Automation: A Perfect Match, p. 61, available: https://www.researchgate.net/profile/Jerome-Geyer-Klingeberg/publication/326466901_Process_Mining_and_Robotic_Process_Automation_A_Perfect_Match/links/5b4f787ea6fdcc8dae2b378c/Process-Mining-and-Robotic-Process-Automation-A-Perfect-Match.pdf, 8.8.2021.

From the process recording, in the sense of the BPM standard, a description is created that is linked to the data (*see* Figure 6.3).

Figure 6.3 Purchasing Process Example

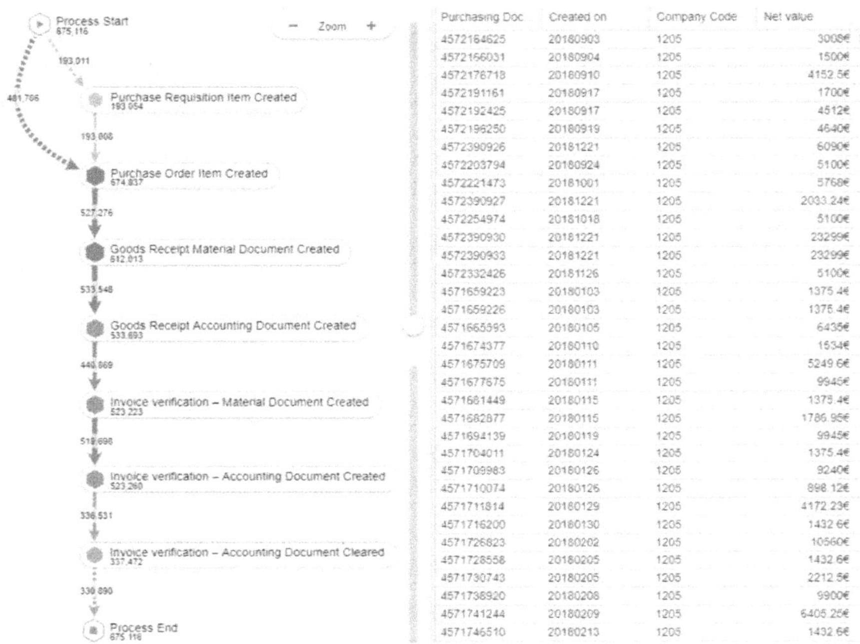

Purchasing Doc	Created on	Company Code	Net value
4572164625	20180903	1205	3008€
4572166031	20180904	1205	1500€
4572176718	20180910	1205	4152.5€
4572191161	20180917	1205	1700€
4572192425	20180917	1205	4512€
4572196250	20180919	1205	4640€
4572390926	20181221	1205	6090€
4572203794	20180924	1205	5100€
4572221473	20181001	1205	5768€
4572390927	20181221	1205	2033.24€
4572254974	20181018	1205	5100€
4572390930	20181221	1205	23299€
4572390933	20181221	1205	23299€
4572332426	20181126	1205	5100€
4571659223	20180103	1205	1375.4€
4571659226	20180103	1205	1375.4€
4571665593	20180105	1205	6435€
4571674377	20180110	1205	1534€
4571675709	20180111	1205	5249.6€
4571677675	20180111	1205	9945€
4571681449	20180115	1205	1375.4€
4571682877	20180115	1205	1786.95€
4571694139	20180119	1205	9945€
4571704011	20180124	1205	1375.4€
4571709983	20180126	1205	9240€
4571710074	20180126	1205	898.12€
4571711814	20180129	1205	4172.23€
4571716200	20180130	1205	1432.6€
4571726823	20180202	1205	10560€
4571728558	20180205	1205	1432.6€
4571730743	20180205	1205	2212.5€
4571738920	20180208	1205	9900€
4571741244	20180209	1205	6405.25€
4571746510	20180213	1205	1432.6€

The output process recording is either implicit or explicit in the form of a process diagram describing the normative process best in BMP(N)[15] (*see* Figure 6.4).

15. Cleiton dos Santos Garcia, Alex Meincheim, Elio Ribeiro Faria Junior, Marcelo Rosano Dallagassa, Denise Maria Vecino Sato, Deborah Ribeiro Carvalho, Eduardo Alves Portela Santos, Edson Emilio Scalabrin, Process mining techniques and applications –A systematic mapping study, Expert Systems With Applications 133 (2019), p 260–295, 265.

Figure 6.4 Fundamentals of Business Process Management (2018)

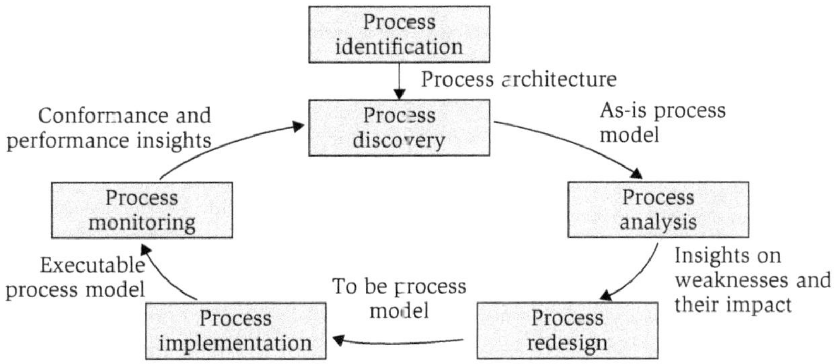

Source: Marlon Dumas, Marcello La Rosa, Jan Mendling & Hajo A. Reijers, *Fundamentals of Business Process Management*, 2nd edn (2018).

The necessity for process management and the associated process modeling consists in the explanation, definition, and specification of the operational processes. Different levels can be distinguished. The tasks to be completed, within the scope of fulfilling the control function, have a law-based complexity, which makes a structured and systematic approach to the design necessary. Process management tasks are:

- Determining boundaries/delimitation of the subject matter: which activities and tasks are to be considered or which are explicitly not considered?
- Determining the subtasks, their sequence and prerequisite.
- Determining the necessary data dependencies, and others.

The above-mentioned points can also be understood as a subsumption technique of tax laws. Tax law facts can be mapped in this way.

In order to implement tax laws in terms of processes, there are various concepts, methods, and techniques of process management, which should be used, whenever the tasks have exceeded a certain limit of complexity.

In addition to understanding the normative process execution, a general understanding of the associated process risks must also be gained. The process risks, in turn, trigger internal control settings. Although this first step cannot reveal every single risk and its associated control, understanding the most important risks is an essential part of understanding the normative process and its controls.

4.1.1 Procurement Process (Purchase to Pay, P2P)

A simple normative model for the P2P process is shown in Figure 6.5.[16]

16. *See* Michael Werner, Financial Process Mining, s. 6 ff. most common example for process mining for financial process flows, pp. 66 ff.; Mieke Jans, Marzie Hosseinpour, How Active Learning

An example of a process risk may be the execution of a purchase order without any approval. This general level of understanding of process risk and the associated controls are necessary to perform the process. It is important to note that the normative model only captures the perspective of the existence and sequence of activities. Perspectives on who does what, implied value, or other aspects not related to the presence or sequence of activities are not included in this notation.

Figure 6.5 Purchase to Pay (P2P) Process

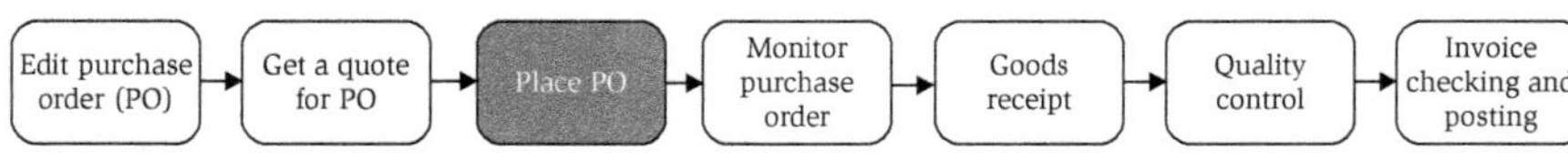

At the same time, various tax and customs subprocesses can be assigned to the procurement process. In the process step "Place purchase order (PO)", the parameters for the VAT / sales tax, customs law, or other tax assessment of the process, are determined.

From the VAT, process mining assessment consists of different process parts that grow together in a so-called end-to-end consideration. Different requirements arise from the various process steps, which reveal further optimization possibilities in a detailed process description. The question to arise is: How can individual process steps be optimized? By using process mining, the recorded and modeled processes can be checked in BPM format for their correct execution (*see* Figure 6.6).

Figure 6.6 Display of Process Deviations

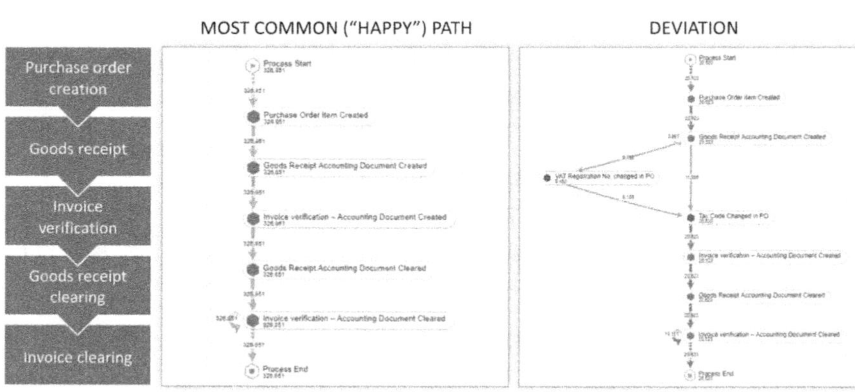

As shown in Figure 6.6, the process chain on the left is called the "happy path." This process is represented by means of process mining with the creation of the order, as the process start, and the sending of the invoice after delivery, as the process end. It

and Process Mining Can Act as Continuous Auditing Catalyst, International Journal of Accounting Information Systems 32 (2019) pp. 44–58, 48.

is called the "happy path" as it is a lean and accurate process flow. If the process deviates in one step, as for example, by changing the VAT registration number after the order has been created, there is an "interruption" in the process flow, represented as a pike. This "deviation" can be a significant source of error, leading to a slowdown in the process or the need for process improvement.

How detailed does a process description need to be? The process description can be used to determine the potential for optimization. Therefore, in the process steps, the data sources should always already be specified in detail, when modeling the processes. This approach facilitates the automation of the processes or the individual process steps, by the various applications The subprocesses in VAT mentioned 3 in the end-to-end consideration can be described as follows:

- VAT ID number query in B2B business—master data—.
- Regular inbound and outbound confirmation of the EU VAT identification number (VAT ID) leads to qualifying validity of the VAT ID number, as well as verification of customer/supplier names and addresses. Automation of these process steps can be done by an RPA or for control purposes by a BI report.
- Order or contract production—master data "bill of material"?

Checking the "bill of material" regarding a percentage of provided material/supplier material is essential for determining the VAT, according to the place of performance. Based on the percentage of the various materials should be determined, whether it is a supply or service, with the corresponding VAT consequences. The maintenance of the tax indicator for the materials (contract manufacturing or only a manufacturing service) leads to a corresponding percentage of provided material. Identification of exceptions and misclassification of tax consequences ensures risk mitigation. Implementation of the checks in the process of creating the bill of materials, default values are automatically transferred to the material master and must be confirmed by the buyer. The evaluation of existing master data by percentage and tax indicator, output right/wrong is based on reading master records. The technology for the check could be an anomaly detection, which detects the mentioned deviations. A combination of the different techniques is feasible, in this regard.

For export/EU intra-community deliveries, the Combined Nomenclature (CN) numbers[17] are important for the transaction implementation in customs. The selection of the delivery terms, by means of the so-called Incoterms,[18] determines the documentation requirements for VAT and customs. When is which process triggered? Which proofs have to be provided, who delivers what? The CN number is used for tax determination and tax rate changes in terms of the master data.[19] All goods that can appear as commercial goods in cross-border traffic are listed in this customs tariff scheme, that is, each good is assigned a specific CN number. The basis for smooth and

17. For further explanation: https://ec.europa.eu/taxation_customs/business/calculation-customs-duties/customs-tariff/combined-nomenclature_en.
18. See for further explanation:https://forto com/de/blog/incoterms-and-when-to-use-which-one/.
19. The customs tariff is a systematically structured list of goods, a so-called Combined Nomenclature (CN number).

uniform clearance is the correct classification of goods in the customs tariff. The tariff classification takes place in the import area in the form of the coding of the goods description up to the 11-digit code number and for market regulation purposes also beyond that, or in the export area up to the 8-digit goods number. Each individual code number contains customs duty rates, the measure for the amount of customs duty incurred. In addition to the determination of duty rates, other legal consequences associated with the cross-border movement of goods can be derived.

Prohibitions and restrictions are:

- import or export requires a permit or license;
- separate foreign trade statistics are required;
- further customs treatment is subject to submission of additional documentation;
- certain actions at the customs are subject to notification;
- the goods are subject to anti-dumping regulations; or
- the use of a duty suspension is possible.

The direct Community legal basis of the Customs Tariff is Regulation (EEC) No. 2658/87 on the tariff and statistical nomenclature and on the Common Customs Tariff. It established the Combined Nomenclature (CN) as the binding customs tariff nomenclature and statistical nomenclature, and is directly applicable in every EU Member State. Article 12 of the regulation stipulates that the European Commission must publish the complete version of the CN together with the tariff rates, every year, in order to ensure that it is permanently up to date. The basis of the 11-digit code number is the Harmonized System (hence the term HS code), which is administered by the World Customs Organization (WCO) and defines the first 6 digits of the code number. The HS is used to designate and code goods with the aim of ensuring the same classification of goods worldwide. Based on this six-digit code, the HS is extended by two digits by the Combined Nomenclature (CN) of the European Community (digits 7 + 8 of the code number). During import clearance, tariff rates, textile categories, prohibitions and restrictions, or import permit facts can be assigned on the basis of this eight-digit number. The ninth and tenth digits (so-called TARIC = Integrated Tariff of the European Community) encode Community measures, such as anti-dumping regulations, tariff suspensions or tariff quotas.

The eleventh digit of the code number is used for national purposes and is used, for example, to encode VAT rates or national prohibitions and restrictions. In an import declaration, the 11-digit code number must always be indicated; in the export declaration, only the 8-digit commodity code number, which can also be taken from the list of goods for foreign trade statistics, must be indicated.

Based on these regulations, the following information is essential:

> *Credit notes and material master:* – Classification of whether a credit note invoice is a price adjustment or a service of the customer (service of the customers in B2B). Identification whether it is an input service or charge reduction. Control of the final credit note creation. Machine learning can be done from the existing transactions and reporting of anomaly detection.

Intrastat reporting: – Reconciliation of advance tax returns with statistical reports, such as Intrastat, automate explanations for time variances, reconciliation with SSC on TSPs used.
Import VAT Reporting: – Is the import VAT recorded as input tax in the correct country in each case or recorded as a cost? The CN number does not contain this information.

4.1.2 Further Examples

- *Incoterms changes with an impact on European sales tax (see Figure 6.7)*
  The contractual terms and conditions under civil law and for VAT purposes for deliveries of raw materials, for example, are defined at the time of the "Place PO" process step. The Incoterms determine who has to pay which costs for transport, customs clearance and any import VAT. If the Incoterms are changed, in the process flow, after the process step "Place PO", and the invoice in the process step "Invoice verification and posting" contains a different Incoterm, this can result in an incorrect VAT refund, due to the assertion of an input tax. The event log is, therefore, the Incoterm in the process step "Place PO", which must be the same as the Incoterm in the received invoice.

Figure 6.7 Incoterms Breakdown: Obligations of the Buyer and Seller[20]

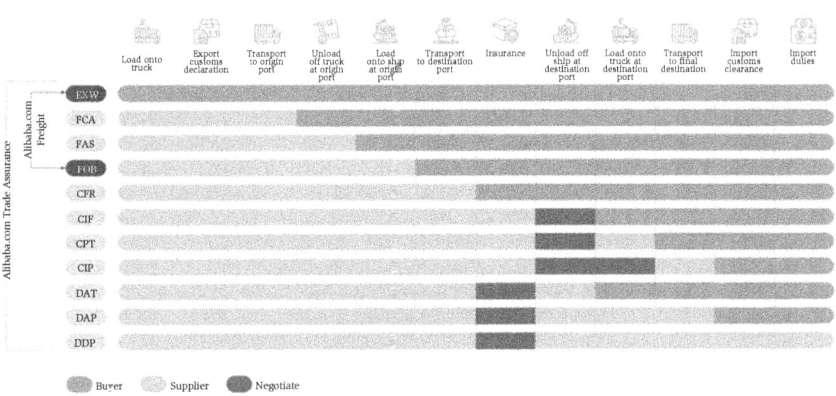

If the Incoterm DAP is used as Delivery at Place, it means: in case of a delivery based on DAP, the seller shall be responsible for the delivery of the goods including the transport costs to the named place of destination at the buyer's premises. Expressly

20. See for further details: https://seller.alibaba.com/businessblogs/px577140-incoterms-guide, viewed 3.8.2021.

excluded are the costs for the completion of all necessary import formalities. These shall be borne by the buyer. Therefore, all charges, customs duties, and import VAT related to the import, in the country of destination, shall be borne by the buyer or the consignee of the goods. The seller's invoice does not include customs duties or invoiced import VAT.

If, on the other hand, the Incoterm is changed to DDP (Delivered Duty Paid), the seller must deliver the goods at their own expense and risk to a destination in the importing country, completing all necessary formalities and bearing all costs and import duties. DDP corresponds to DAP in terms of content, plus customs and tax handling. What does this mean for the foreign customer? The customer does not have to pay anything when receiving the shipment, the goods are delivered like a national shipment. In this variant, the sender has the goods cleared by a partner in the EU. An invoice from the seller would show an import VAT, although, it is not owed according to the contractual terms. Such an invoice would be incorrect, and the recipient of the goods would claim the import VAT, which was usually not paid as input tax, in his advance VAT return.

- *Source and destination changes of a delivery of goods*
  If the delivery routes of the ordered goods are changed, after the contract has been concluded, for example, because production facilities are no longer able to deliver during the COVID-19 pandemic, this has an impact on the customs assessment of the country of origin, as well as for VAT purposes. Identifying such changes in the purchasing process is, therefore, essential.

Further use cases in connection with customs duties and sales taxes are:

- Invoice postings without goods receipt.
- Cancellations of invoices with changed VAT tax codes.
- Services with goods tax code, as in the case of differentiation between work deliveries and work services.
- Goods returns with incorrect debit notes.

4.1.3 Withholding Tax Deductions

The described use cases from the procurement process do not require any further process steps or subprocesses that are tested with process mining. More complex tax regulations, such as the legal requirements for WHT, require further details or subprocesses to the main process "ordering process." The purchase of marketing services from artists, bloggers, or influencers, with limited tax liability, in Germany, results in the deduction of a withholding tax from the agreed fee for tax purposes.

Section 50a (1), of the German Income Tax Act (EStG), formulates the basic rule of the taxation procedure, in the case of limited tax liability, by establishing a tax withholding obligation for four groups of domestic income. By way of example, a process is shown from the first group.

Section 50a (2) No. 1: Income from artistic, sporting, artistic, entertainment, or similar performances, subject to limited tax liability, in Germany, within the meaning of Section 49 (1) Nos. 2 to 4, 9 EStG, is hereinafter, referred to as performance income. In the case of limited tax liability, a tax withholding obligation shall be imposed. The tax withholding obligation is imposed irrespective of the type of income. Incidentally, the provision contains the obligation of the party liable for payment (customer) to clarify the tax residency of its contractual partner. This is because the addressees of the provision are ultimately the performers without domestic residency criteria and their contractual partners.

Although the party liable for payment will regularly be subject to unlimited tax liability, in Germany, domestic residency is not a requirement of the provision.

Section 50a (1) EStG: For an activity carried out by a natural person, in Germany, the tax rate on the gross income is 15%; if a net income agreement is made, the rate is 30%. The tax deduction, as withholding tax, can be avoided for the performer by submitting a so-called exemption certificate to the orderer, which they have to apply for at the German Federal Central Office (BZSt). Foreign artists, athletes, licensors, and supervisory boards (remuneration creditors) can apply to the BZSt for relief, from German withholding tax, under section 50a of the German Income Tax Act (EStG), if a double taxation agreement (DTA) provides for full or partial exemption from withholding tax, in Germany, for income earned, in Germany.

The process presented with BPM has the subprocess of handling the steps around the withholding tax exemption or obligation. The contractual conditions are also essential, which can lead to different assessments with or without withholding tax, and at which tax rate, 15% or 30%. In addition, for example, in the relationship with bloggers or influencers, there will not always be a contractual relationship in written form. This means that for the further subprocess step, a questionnaire for the missing written contractual agreement will be necessary to verify the verbally concluded contractual terms. Thus, only after clarification and presentation of the exemption certificate, can it be decided how to create the order in the main process. If no exemption certificate is available, the withholding tax key must be determined and inserted into the order process. Furthermore, at the end of the process, with the payment of the invoice, the tax certificate is created, in case of withholding tax deduction for the service recipient. The orderer now has all the data to create the tax declaration according to section 50a EStG (*see* Figure 6.8).

Figure 6.8 BPM for Section 50a(1) No. 1 German Income Tax Act

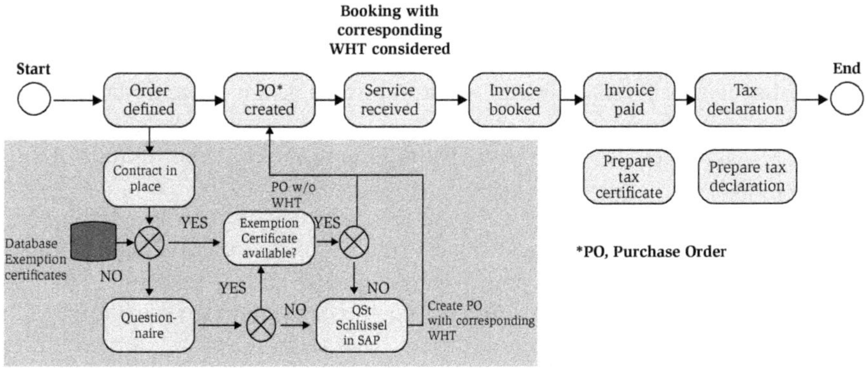

4.1.4 Withholding Tax Outside the Purchase Order Process

Withholding taxes, outside the purchase order process, are usually associated with Articles 10, 11 and 12 OECD DTA MA, with dividends, royalties, and interest, subject to withholding tax, in the source country. According to the mentioned provisions of the double taxation treaty, these withholding taxes can be reduced to a low percentage.

In the presentation of a dividend process (*see* Figure 6.9), the issue is whether the rules of the double taxation treaty for the possible reduction of withholding tax have been observed in the process step "Determine the right WHT rate." This requires additional verification steps, which can also be performed with process mining.

Figure 6.9 Dividend Distribution Process Illustration for German Legal Entities

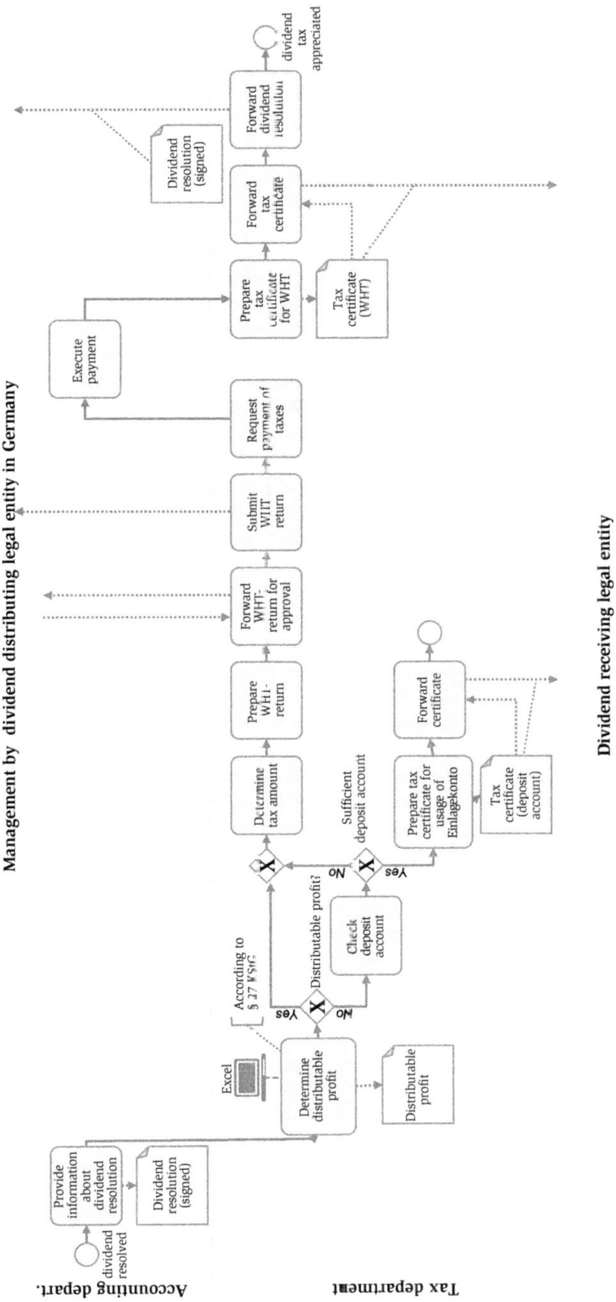

As already explained in the introduction, process mining can be applied to processes already described, as well as to processes yet to be identified. A qualitative examination takes place. In section 4.1.1, a deviation of the target process from the actual process can be determined, further steps must be performed.

4.2 Second Step: Availability of Transaction Data

The second step is to extract the transactions of the process under investigation from the ERP or information system. A traditional selection of purchasing process data is a list of some purchase orders and associated invoices, regardless of whether this process is examined through analytics or manually.

Table 6.1 shows two example lists that could be the result of the second step. An automated check of all data would contain all relevant orders and invoices of the examined period.

Table 6.1 Transnational Data Display, According to Mieke Jans, Marzie Hosseinpour[21]

Transactional data.

Purchase Order

Nr.	Date	Value	Signed	Released	Goods received	Invoice
An example list of a purchase orders for internal control testing						
1	Sep. 1, 2016	23,300	☑	☑	☑	101
2	Sep. 1, 2016	7329	☑	☑	☑	102
3	Sep. 1, 2016	2090	☐	☑	☐	103
4	Sep. 1, 2016	4675	☑	☑	☑	104
5	Sep. 1, 2016	135	☐	☑	☐	105
6	Sep. 1, 2016	4500	☑	☑	☐	106
7	Sep. 1, 2016	7210	☑	☐	☑	107
8	Sep. 1, 2016	69,023	☑	☑	☑	108
9	Sep. 1, 2016	12,000	☑	☑	☑	109
10	Sep. 1, 2016	40,329	☑	☑	☑	110

Invoice

Nr.	Purchase order	Date	Value
An example list of invoices for internal control testing			
101	1	Sep. 12, 2016	23,300
102	2	Sep. 14, 2016	7329
103	3	Sep. 2, 2016	2090
104	4	Sep. 20, 2016	4675
105	5	Sep. 4, 2016	135
106	6	Sep. 25, 2016	4500
107	7	Sep. 18, 2016	3605
108	8	Sep. 29, 2016	69,023
109	9	Sep. 19, 2016	120,052
110	10	Sep. 11, 2016	40,329
111		Sep. 15, 2016	67

The data from the information system have different components. Qualitative data as "signed," "released" and "goods received", which represent so-called metadata, is essential. Metadata or meta-information is structured data that contain information about other information resources. Metadata, thus, describes the actual

21. As an example of the basic representation is the representation nach Mieke Jans, Marzie Hosseinpour, How Active Learning and Process Mining Can Act as Continuous Auditing Catalyst, International Journal of Accounting Information Systems 32 (2019) pp. 44-58, 48.

data in an additional way. Meta-information becomes necessary when there are larger amounts of data to manage. A pronounced characteristic of metadata is, therefore, that it is often machine-readable and analyzable. How retailers store information about their products and their customers, this is all considered as metadata. Metadata is information that is created, stored, and shared, to describe things. It allows us to interact with these things in order to obtain the knowledge needed. The classic definition is literal, based on the etymology of the word itself, meaning, "data about data." With this broad definition, it would be expected that metadata could be found everywhere, and in fact it is.[22]

Metadata, for the ordering process, is the use of Incoterms for ordering and invoicing, or in the withholding tax process, according to section 50a EStG, the existence of the exemption certificate, the determination of the withholding tax rate. Metadata can be text annotations, written in a machine-readable language, that assigns meaning to individual numbers, words, passages, or documents. In a double tax treaty, the withholding tax rate for free float dividends is identifiable to the computer by an additional piece of information, marker, or referred to as a "tag." Such metadata includes information about the specific rules that make automatable processing possible.[23]

4.3 Third Step: Identify Deviations by Comparing Transactions Against the Normative Process

In a third step, the normative process and the available transaction data are compared. If the transaction or the process execution preceding the transaction matches the expected normative model, there is evidence of safety. If the transaction deviates from what is expected, the deviation is stored in a separate list. Comparing the transaction data at hand, shown in the Transaction Data table (Table 6.1), with the normative model in Figure 6.2, it appears that orders 1, 2, 4, 8, 9, and 10 meet the expectations of the normative model. According to the information, these purchase orders have been signed, released, goods receipt has occurred, and an associated invoice is available. In terms of compliance with the normative model, these purchase orders do not appear to deviate. The remaining purchase orders are listed as a deviation. Invoice number 111 is also listed as a deviation because no associated purchase order was submitted.

If this initial investigation were not limited to the activities performed and the other information were also considered, purchase Order No 9 would be listed as a deviation, that is, the value on the associated invoice is slightly higher than on the purchase order. This may be caused by other cost elements that were not included in the purchase order, such as possibly transportation costs or customs duties or sales tax. The scope of the elements that are considered, when performing this third step,

22. Jenn Riley, Understanding Metadata, retrievable: https://www.fidgeo.de/wp-content/uploads/2016/07/2017_01-NISO-understanding-metadata.pdf, 5.08.2021.
23. Heribert Anzinger, Möglichkeiten der Digitalisierung des Rechts in Drüen, Digitalisierung im Steuerrecht, DStJG 2018, pp. 15–58, 30.

depends on the procedure used in the verification steps; that is, are all elements to be included at once or is the investigation divided into several parts.

For clarity, the example is limited to examining only the Process flow in this step. Other business rules such as "The value of a purchase order should be equal to the value of the invoice," the use of Incoterms, the purchase of goods in the sense of a goods receipt, and so on, must each be examined separately.

4.3.1 Analysis of the Deviation List

Based on the listed deviations of the second step, these deviations must be classified. In the procedure, there are three possible outcomes:

> *Exception:* A first possibility is that the transaction deviates from the normative model, but this deviation is also a valid process execution. In the example presented in Table 6.1, invoice 111 deviates from the normative model, because it is not associated with a purchase order. Although it is not ideal from a risk perspective to procure items without a purchase order, this is an accepted deviation. Such deviations often occur in a company; however, the causes need to be determined and investigated. For example, it could be the case when ordering flowers to thank an employee, or other smaller, quick expenditures. Deviations that are accepted and serve to provide the necessary flexibility to react quickly and work effectively are called exceptions or so-called tolerable exceptions. In the use case of Incoterms changes, this means that the contract, the purchase order must be adjusted accordingly, to allow the control of the sales tax codes in the ERP system to run correctly in the process flow. Subsequent changes from a purchase order transaction to final invoices should, therefore, be strictly tracked within the various process steps or "flagged" from exception in the future. The algorithm can learn this exception and flag it as "OK" in case of a new process control.
>
> There will be few exceptions in tax and customs law. Tax processes are based on statutory factual requirements that must be met. Exceptions are usually a violation of tax compliance, if they are not provided for in the law.
>
> *Anomaly:* A second possibility is that the deviation is classified as an anomaly, as "an undesirable deviation." These deviations are classified as anomalies and added to the list of anomalies that warrant further investigation. An example may be a purchase order that was not released, such as in Table 6.1, purchase order 7, but the goods were received along with an invoice (107). The release of the purchase order is a company-specific control that becomes relevant for tax purposes only if it is also provided for by law. Fiscally, it was not an anomaly for sales tax purposes. The characteristics of a taxable supply would be met, as soon as the goods are received, even without the purchase order release.
>
> In the dividend process, the receipt of the dividend, after deduction of the maximum withholding tax, would be the regular process. The withholding tax reduction, under double tax treaties, would not have occurred, which is

potentially an anomaly, if the withholding tax reduction is available under the actual facts. For example, the metadata reference under the DTA rules is missing in this case. In this particular case, the requirements for the tax reduction must be examined separately. In the withholding tax deduction procedure, according to section 50a EStG, the question arises as to whether the exemption certificate is valid and has been correctly submitted, or whether the correct tax rate has been used for posting in the absence of an exemption certificate.

Potential compliance issue: The third possibility is that although the process deviation cannot be resolved immediately, the manual review would resolve this deviation. Returning to the normative procurement model and data example in the source example (4.1.1), purchase orders 3 and 5 are listed as a deviation because a signature is missing. However, the auditor could identify the underlying business rule that states that purchase orders under 200 do not need to be signed. To reach a final classification of the discrepancy, the hypothesis "order value is less than 200" must be tested. Without evidence to support the hypothesis, the deviation is classified as a potential compliance issue. In the case of this third possibility, the internal control review process continues. If no deviations are classified in this category, the internal control review is completed when the "Deviations Classified" state is reached. The output is a list of anomalies that warrant further investigation. Based on the deviations that indicate a potential compliance issue, a follow-up investigation is specified. The specifications relate to the potential risk and the identified business rule that, if effective, would mitigate that risk. For example, the follow-up investigation might relate to the risk of missing signatures on high-value purchases. The agreed-upon business rule might be "if the purchase value is less than 200, no signature is required." In this case, the follow-up investigation could be specified to verify that all purchases missing a signature actually have a purchase value of less than 200.

While the "process" is seen as a holistic concept, a "rule" is narrowed down to a few specific characteristics, such as the value of a purchase and the presence or absence of a signature. In the baseline example (Table 6.1), the transactions under consideration (those without signatures, such as orders 3 and 5) would be tested to see if they have a value that is less than 200. If this is not the case (as in the case of order No. 3), the transaction ends up back on the list of discrepancies, and a new cycle of "Analyze List of Discrepancies" follows.

In tax and customs law, there is a need, based on the legal requirements, to implement the laws in a machine-readable form. In essence, this would mean that in tax law, a clear determination of the programming language would be necessary. Machine-readable laws would not, however, necessarily have to be based on principles mounted legislation waiver around certain legal concepts, and discretionary standards are still possible. Principles and discretionary rules, thus, do not escape algorithmization. Type terms in juristic systems can be connected technically with pattern explanation procedures. This means that in the interpretation of the type term, the need of an above-mentioned deviation can occur, which is accessible to a subsequent change by the examiner. An example of this is the tax characteristics for a so-called co-partnership of a partnership. The partner under civil law must bear a co-entrepreneurial initiative and a co-entrepreneurial risk, in order to fulfill the facts of Section 15 (1) sentence 1 no. 2 EStG, as a taxable co-entrepreneurship for tax purposes. The characteristics of the initiative and the risk can be pronounced to different degrees, which opens up the aforementioned scope for assessment.

In addition, the exercise of administrative discretion can be automated. On this basis, the legislature could create a system of Big Data-driven Legal Personalization [24] and define it as a new approach in the automated implementation of legislation. In the literature on tax compliance, in particular through Ayres/Braithwaite[25] the option of "Responsive Regulation" describes a new form of tax compliance implementation. This form of implementation, of tax law, promotes voluntary tax compliance and the question of how to interpret tax laws in the case of value concepts that need to be filled in.[26]

The discussion on the undefined legal terms, of a type concept or administrative discretion, shows that a further examination procedure may be necessary in the context of process mining; that is, not every anomaly is to be recognized as such.

The three possibilities of "exception," "anomaly," and "potential compliance issue" are ultimately revisited as part of the process mining process. If the purchase remains above 200, but does not show a signature, a new potential compliance problem can be identified along with a newly formulated hypothesis. For example, "if the supplier is on the 'trusted supplier' list, no signature is required." Then the process continues with testing this hypothesis and so on. The same can be done for the fiscal terms mentioned above.

4.3.2 Event Log

The starting point for process mining is an event log. The basic assumptions of this protocol are that it is possible to have such a set of events that:

- each event refers to a task [...];
- each event refers to a case [...]; and
- the events are completely ordered.

Each occurrence of an activity is a unique event. An event log contains more information than just transactional data; it contains the data about data described earlier, called metadata. This allows the event log to show temporal dependencies

24. Siehe im Privatrecht Grigoleit, AcP 218, 2018, 601 (604, Fn 5, Busch, Granular legal norms: Big Data and the Personalization of Private Law, in Mak/Tjong/tai,Berle (Hrsg.), research Handbook on Data of Private Law, 2018, 408.
25. Ayres/Braithwaite,Responsive Regulation, 1992, Siehe auch P.Fettke/ R.Risse, DB 2018, 1748/1748f); Self-Driving Laws, Casey/Niblett, Self-Driving Laws, University of Toronto Law Journal 66, 2016, 429.
26. Looschelders/Roth, Juristische Methodik im Prozess der Rechtsfindung, S. 198.

between activities. For example, instead of just knowing that goods were received (checked box), it is possible to retrieve when and how often goods were received.

Table 6.2 Event Logs as Metadata, Display According to Mieke Jans, Marzie Hosseinpour[27]

A selection of first 10 process executions of a procurement process.

Purch. order	Event 1	Event 2	Event 3	Event 4	Event 5	Event 6	Event 7	...
1	Create PO	Sign	Release	Goods receipt	Invoice receipt	Pay		
2	Create PO	Sign	Release	Goods receipt	Invoice receipt	Pay		
3	Create PO	Release	Invoice receipt	Pay				
4	Create PO	Sign	Release	Goods receipt	Invoice receipt	Pay	Pay	
5	Create PO	Release	Invoice receipt	Pay				
6	Create PO	Sign	Release	Invoice receipt	Pay			
7	Create PO	Sign	Invoice receipt	Goods receipt	Pay			
8	Create PO	Change line	Sign	Release	Goods receipt	Invoice receipt	Pay	
9	Create PO	Sign	Release	Invoice receipt	Goods receipt	Pay		
10	Create PO	Sign	Release	Goods receipt	Invoice receipt	Pay		

Table 6.2 is an example of a simplified event log that could have been created from the transaction data in the previous example (Transaction Data table). Note that the event log contains six activities (related to the rectangles in Table 6.1), but 56 unique occurrences of the activities (6 + 5 + 4 + 7 + 4 + 5 + 5 + 7 + 6 + 6), called events. In an audit context, the events, in an event log, typically refer to transactions involving documents, such as the release of a purchase order. This example log uses only the temporal ordering of events and abstracts from other characteristics, such as value, vendor, and document number.

From an event log, it is possible to gain a better view of process flows. A trace is a unique sequence of events that is executed to complete the process.

In the example in Table 6.2, a trace consists of all events mentioned in a line. Thus, orders 1, 2, 4, and 10 share the same trace, as do orders 3 and 5. To structure the transaction data, in an event log, there must be a timestamp for each event, along with a link to a "common case."

A "case," or "process instance" as this is called, could be an invoice, a purchase order, a blogger service, a cross-border shipment of goods, or a dividend receipt. It is the unique identifier that connects different events in a process execution (as in a purchase).

Beyond these minimal requirements, an event log can store additional information. This may relate to the resource (a particular person or system) that performed the activity, or to other data elements, such as the transaction value. Although the additional information is not mandatory, from a technical point of view, for process mining, it is crucial from the point of view of subsequent auditing of deviations; that is, subsequent compliance checks.

27. Mieke Jans, Marzie Hosseinpour, How Active Learning and Process Mining Can Act as Continuous Auditing Catalyst, International Journal of Accounting Information Systems 32 (2019) pp. 44-58.

The discovery of real process executions, in the form of event sequences, without details on persons involved, invoice numbers, information on the legal facts, as in the case of withholding tax, according to section 50a EStG, and transactions, will not provide substantial audit evidence.

The generic internal control audit procedure must be clearly presented. This makes it possible to present a framework that uses available data and process mining techniques for transactional verification. This results in three requirements for the framework for process mining use:

- Transactional verification starts with the business process.
- Alert management is critical to make the approach actionable.
- A human expert is used as an "oracle" to combine human and computer intelligence to classify transactions.
- The system takes a two-stage approach to the applied perspective.
- In a first stage, only the control flow perspective is used. Transactions are considered in the context of their process execution, and only the sequence of activities is considered.
- Only in the second stage, when additional data is required to classify transactions as anomaly or not, the data perspective is added. This perspective brings information such as the value, the person, and so on, into the equation.
- The first four phases are part of the control flow perspective.
- The following last two phases 5 and 6 are in the data perspective.

5 CONCLUSION

In summary, the phases in the application of process mining can be described as follows:

Phase 1

First, the transaction data, of the process under consideration, is extracted from the corresponding relational database. The data from this database is then converted into an event log. This event log is used as input for a compliance check phase.

Phase 2

In the second phase, a conformance checking algorithm is applied to compare the real transaction data, in the event log, with the normative process model. The normative process model can be represented either procedurally or declaratively.

The former is a graphical description of how process executions should proceed, and the latter is a description of what must be executed, along with constraints typically formulated in a set of business rules. If a process execution respects these constraints, the execution shall conform to the model.

The system assumes a procedural process model that strictly postulates the sequence of activities that must be followed. This normative model, together with the event log, is used as input to a conformance checking algorithm. This conformance check considers only the order of activities and abstracts from additional constraints. The output, of this phase, is a list of deviations related to the process flows. The deviations identified, in this phase, are process executions that differ from what is captured in the normative process model.

Phase 3

The list of deviations will contain three types of process executions: executions that are perfect, even if they deviate from the normative model (OK); those that cannot be justified under any circumstances (NOK); and those for which more information is needed to classify them. Because the list of deviations is based only on the control-flow perspective, the classification of some cases is inconsistent, as noted in the group. The term "inconsistent" refers to the inconsistent behavior of the final classification to which the cases belong: one time a sequence is OK, another time the same sequence is NOK, depending on additional features.

Given the design of the system to assume only a control-flow perspective, the inclusion of a classifier that can handle inconsistency, is inherent to this system. These are called flexible classification models, which support the inclusion of further knowledge from human experts.

In simpler terms, an active learning model, for audit environments, should be able to distinguish between safe and unacceptable transactions.

However, for borderline transactions, the system should delegate responsibility to the human experts, learning from their rational decisions. Instead of an algorithm being forced to assign this transaction to one of the two classes (OK or NOK), it pushes this case further to the expert. This behavior resembles real-world scenarios much better than a binary yes/no scenario. In practice, experts prefer intelligent systems that can collaborate with them to establish a knowledge relationship between humans and machines.

Phase 4

In the fourth phase, the classifier is fed with the complete list of deviations, without the labeled sample. The output is again a combination of three "lists." The "OK" list contains deleted deviations that leave the test procedure. The "NOK" list goes directly to the list of anomalies for further investigation in a subsequent stage. The deviations where the algorithm was unsure go to the second stage, which uses additional data.

Phase 5

The deviations that could not be classified, by the classifier, are enriched with additional data. Only here, when additional information is needed to make a final classification, the framework turns to the data perspective.

Phase 6

A human expert will act as a so-called oracle and present rules that could eliminate the rule deviation. For example: an invoice without a purchase order, an exemption certificate and withholding tax according to section 50a EStG, or without Incoterms.

The oracle presents the related rule(s) that could justify this deviation. For example, rule if the supplier is listed as a trusted supplier, no purchase order is needed. Data regarding the supplier of the deviating process curve is added to the process-related data and the deviation is tested against this rule. An expert provides any rules that could potentially justify the deviant behavior, and these rules are tested at this stage. The result is a final clearance of the deviation, or an additional anomaly on the list that warrants further investigation.

This final classification is also used as additional input to the classifier, which is now given more human-based knowledge to learn from, and will eventually produce fewer and fewer deviations in the "unsafe" category in Phase 4.

The option of immediately acquiring all rules from the human expert and programming them, is thought-provoking. We postulate that it is difficult, if at all feasible, for the expert to provide a complete set of rules with 100% certainty. By confronting the expert with variations in the activity sequence, implicit knowledge about which rule is activated, in which activity sequence, is extracted and made explicit. The more often a rule is presented in different situations, the higher the confidence level of that rule. In this way, human expertise can be captured.

Traditional process mining algorithms use the time dependencies, between recorded events, to infer the control flow. These are not suitable for financially relevant data, recorded in ERP systems, where recorded events are not yet matched to cases, and where these cases are non-linear. The process mining method, in accounting, uses the data structure dependencies of recorded events rather than the chronological order of the events to derive a control flow.[28]

Process mining is very well suited for control and compliance checks of tax and customs processes. Taxpayers can use this "tool" to make their law enforcement more transparent, save costs and optimize any tax and customs audits.

28. Michael Werner, Financial Process Mining, s. 74.

Index

R

S

T

U

V

W

Z

www.ingramcontent.com/pod-product-compliance
Lightning Source LLC
Chambersburg PA
CBHW070252260926
51849CB00001BA/240
9789403543130